Gramsci's Thought

Gramsci's Thought

E.M.S. Namboodiripad

P. Govinda Pillai

Translated by M.G. Radhakrishnan

First published in May 2021 by
LeftWord Books
2254/2A Shadi Khampur
New Ranjit Nagar
New Delhi 110008
INDIA

LeftWord Books and Vaam Prakashan are imprints of
Naya Rasta Publishers Pvt. Ltd.

First published in Malayalam as *Gramsciyan Vichara Viplavam*
by Chintha Publishers, Thiruvananthapuram, 1996

leftword.com

ISBN   978-81-940778-6-2 (paperback)
          978-81-950310-0-9 (e-book)

Digital print edition, August 2024

CONTENTS

M.G. Radhakrishnan

WHY THIS BOOK

Antonio Gramsci is the most discussed Marxist after Marx, Engels, and Lenin. According to Perry Anderson, no Italian thinker enjoys greater fame today than Gramsci and, if academic citations and internet references are any guide, he is more influential than even Machiavelli.[1] The bibliography of articles and books about him now runs to some 20,000 items.

Gramsci spent over eleven years in Mussolini's fascist prison. He died within days of being released for medical attention. Eight decades after his death at the age of 46 and more than three decades after the implosion of the Communist world, newer books and studies on the scholar-activist and his works continue to be written in various languages all over the world. So much so that 'a veritable cottage industry has churned out countless analyses about this work making it one of the most written about texts in the Marxist tradition', writes Joe Cleffie, with special reference to Gramsci's *Prison Notebooks*.[2] The *Prison Notebooks* were written during

---

[1] Perry Anderson, *The Antinomies of Antonio Gramsci*, London: Verso, 2017.

[2] Joe Cleffie, 'Rescuing Gramsci from his misinterpreters', review of *The Gramscian Moment: Philosophy, Hegemony and Marxism*, by Peter Thomas, *International Socialist Review*, no. 93, June 2012 (https://isreview.org/issue/93/rescuing-gramsci-his-misinterpreters, last accessed 8 July 2019).

Gramsci's years of incarceration and debilitating ailments. Even political and intellectual tendencies with little in common have laid claim to Gramsci's writing. In a 2013 speech, notes George Eaton, Michael Gove – the UK's Education Secretary – cited Gramsci 'in defence of his emphasis on traditional teaching methods'. The French far-right group Nouvelle Droite and its Belgian counterpart Vlaams Belang also claim Gramsci.[3]

There has been a manifold increase in Gramsci's relevance especially in the aftermath of the socialist world's collapse. For most of what had led to the implosion could be traced to his highly original hypotheses on the process of revolution and the sustenance of socialist society post revolution. The complexities of the recent revolutionary and counter-revolutionary processes witnessed in the Middle East too have only elucidated the significance of Gramscian thought and insights.[4] 'In an era of social media, viral videos and mass higher education, Gramsci's concept of hegemony feels startlingly prescient. Indeed, he even more appears not merely a Marxist thinker for our times, but perhaps *the* thinker,' writes Eaton.

In the face of such a mounting body of knowledge and analyses on this thinker-revolutionary-martyr and his thought, what could be the rationale for publishing a little primer on Gramsci, that too written more than two decades ago, in an Indian language – Malayalam – spoken by thirty-three million people? The clue lies not quite in Gramsci but in this book's authors and their politics. E.M.S. Namboodiripad was one of the most prominent leaders and intellectuals of the Communist Party of India (Marxist), India's largest Communist party. P. Govinda Pillai was an outstanding Marxist intellectual of the CPI (M). EMS was

---

[3] George Eaton, 'Why Antonio Gramsci is the Marxist thinker for our times', *New Statesman*, 2 February 2018.

[4] Brecht de Smet, *Gramsci on Tahrir: Revolution and Counter-Revolution in Egypt*, London: Pluto Press, 2016.

a founder member of the Communist Party of India and of the Communist Party of India (Marxist). He was the general secretary of the CPI in 1962, the first Communist chief minister of an Indian state – Kerala (1957–59), and general secretary of the CPI (M) (1977–92). P. Govinda Pillai was a member of the State Committee of the CPI (M) and a Member of the Legislative Assembly of Kerala thrice. He was for many years the chief editor of *Deshabhimani*, the CPI (M)'s Malayalam-language newspaper.

The CPI (M) is one of the very few Communist parties of the world that has survived the socialist bloc's collapse without disowning any of the classical Marxist tenets to which it claims allegiance. The authors could be described as India's two most prominent 'new intellectuals' in the mould of the Gramscian definition and who broke the dividing line between intellectual work and revolutionary activism.[5] Like Gramsci they too firmly believed in the traditional role and relevance of an organized working class party as the vanguard of the revolutionary movement.

Finally, India's current political context bears special significance for Gramsci's thought. The Indian Communist movement is now faced with an unprecedented crisis: the phenomenal ascent of the Bharatiya Janata Party – with its arsenal of fascistic organizations. Gramsci gives us pointers for the rebuilding of the Left.

---

[5] *The New Intellectuals*, Tricontinental: Institute for Social Research Dossier no. 12, February 2019 (https://www.thetricontinental.org/the-new-intellectual/).

Vijay Prashad

ANTONIO GRAMSCI

AS THE PHILOSOPHER OF PRAXIS

In the early 1990s, E.M.S. Namboodiripad (1909–1998) came across the *Prison Notebooks* of Antonio Gramsci (1891–1937). Gramsci, one of the most significant communist theorists of his time, had spent his time in prison writing essays and notes to clarify the situation of the communist revolution in Italy, and the victory of the fascist forces. These writings, written in secret over a decade (1929–1937) largely in the prison of Turi near Bari, were smuggled out by Gramsci's family, preserved by his comrades, and then published first a little over a decade after Gramsci's death. It was P. Govinda Pillai (1926–2012) – known to his comrades as PG – who had first given EMS a volume of Gramsci's *Prison Notebooks*. EMS read part of it and jokingly chided PG for not giving him Gramsci's work to read a decade or more earlier as he found himself astounded by the great quality of the theoretical assessments in it. By now in his early 80s, EMS told PG to write a book about Gramsci in Malayalam. PG said that he would only

Grateful to M.A. Baby, CPI (M) Polit Bureau member, for his encouragement and assistance with this book.

do so if EMS wrote it with him, so the two of them got to work. An early fruit of the reading EMS had done was published in *The Marxist* ('Antonio Gramsci: The Man and his Thoughts', vol. XII, no. 3, July–September 1995). The next year, EMS and PG released a full book on Gramsci's thought in Malayalam (*Gramscian Vichara Viplavam*, 1996). This book – translated by PG's son M.G. Radhakrishnan – is the English version of that effort.

On Gramsci

On 27 April 1937, at the age of 46, Italy's most formidable Communist and Marxist Antonio Gramsci died. Gramsci had been arrested by the fascists in November 1926. At his trial, the public prosecutor said, 'For twenty years we must stop this brain from functioning.' He was wrong. In prison, Gramsci wrote regularly, smuggling out his notes and his ideas – three thousand pages in total – which would eventually be published in 1948; Gramsci is best known for these *Prison Notebooks*.

Born in 1891 in Sardinia, Gramsci had first-hand knowledge of the wretchedness of the agrarian conditions of Italy's southern part; he would later go to university in Turin, the heart of Italy's industrial zone, where he saw the Workers' Council movement first hand; a journalist for the socialist press, he would be a founder of the Italian Communist Party, work in Moscow for the Communist International before he returned to Italy to be thrown in prison.

The main themes of Gramsci's work are evident early in his life. In 1916, he wrote an article entitled 'Socialism and Culture', in which he argued that 'every revolution has been preceded by an intense cultural activity, by cultural penetration, by the penetration of ideas through the gathering of individuals, recalcitrant at first and only concerned with solving their own economic and political problems, day by day, hour by hour, without bonds of solidarity with others enduring the same conditions'. This cultural activity, this deep fight against dangerous hierarchies and habits inherited from the past, had to be conducted on a political basis by a party, not by individuals. This was an early lesson, which drew Gramsci into the socialist movement.

The great gap between peasant Sardinia and industrial Turin haunted him, not only in his famous 1926 essay on 'The Southern Question', but even in his insistence that the 1924 Communist Party paper – *L'Unitá* or *Unity* have as its subtitle the words 'The Workers and Peasants Daily'. In his 1921 essay on the Livorno Congress, he wrote, 'Workers' emancipation can only occur with the alliance between industrial workers of the North and the poor peasants of the South for the overthrow of the bourgeois state and the establishment of the workers' and peasant's state.' Gramsci had great sympathy for Lenin's worker-peasant alliance, which came from his own Sardinian roots and his experience of the worker council movement in Turin. The Turin years were important to Gramsci, since it was there that he absorbed revolutionary possibility from the proletariat of Turin, whom he called in 1920 'the spiritual leader of the Italian working masses'.

On 21 January 1921, Gramsci participated in the founding of the Italian Communist Party; he was elected to its central committee. These were hard days – on the one side the Soviet Revolution was developing, and on the other the fascists were gaining strength in Italy. 'What is fascism if viewed through an international scale?' Gramsci asked. 'It is an attempt to solve the problems of production and exchange with machine guns and rounds of gunfire.' In the debate inside the Italian party, Gramsci took the view that the organization of the working class and peasantry must be the priority, because the weakened people were being destroyed by the fascists. It was too late.

In prison, Gramsci would reflect on why the fascists won and the communists lost in Italy. It was not enough for a communist to seek political power or to make economic demands. They had to understand hegemony – namely that the ruling class rules not merely with coercion but with consent as well; that the Communists must convince the country that their project is legitimate and that they are the authentic leaders of this national project. Ideology needed to be studied, moral claims of the bourgeoisie needed to be contested with an alternative horizon. When the bourgeoisie relies only on force, then there is a crisis of legitimacy; the loss of consent does not immediately transfer consent to the proletariat, rather there is an interregnum, when the 'old dies, but the new is not yet born'. The Communists must – through the Party and outside the Party – engage in full-scale cultural struggle to propose a different vision of culture and life, to settle the dilemmas of humanity on the side of progress. Gramsci's comrade Palmiro Togliatti gave a series of lectures in Moscow to exiled Italian communists in 1935 on fascism; the broad theme of these lectures is for the communists to democratize culture and to build institutions of working-class culture across Italy (*Lectures on Fascism*, 1970). Gramsci's great contribution to our movement is to get us to understand that the fight over morality and ethics, the very horizon of human possibility is a class struggle.

Behind all of Gramsci's assessments of culture and the question of ideology lies the *necessity* of the proletarian revolution. In July 1920, he wrote an article called 'Two Revolutions', which reflected on the revolutionary process during the massive strike waves that shook Northern Italy from April to September; behind this worker unrest lay flat on the floor the failed revolutions in Austria, Bavaria, Germany, Hungary, and Ukraine. Gramsci found that in these European countries, despite the collapse of the bourgeois state, despite the strength of the trade union movement, and despite the active work of the communist party, the revolutionary waves could not succeed. What was missing was the confidence of the industrial workers to conduct the revolution with the factory as their epicentre; what was needed, but lacking, was 'a conscious movement of the proletarian masses to give substance to their political power with economic power, and a determination on the part of these proletarian masses to introduce proletarian order into the factory, to make the factory the nucleus of the new state'.

In the autumn of 1930, while in prison in Bari, Gramsci gave his fellow communist prisoners a series of lectures in the courtyard. Years later, a report on these lectures was written by his fellow Communist Party of Italy member and prisoner, Athos Lisa, and published in *Rinascita* (12 December 1964; translated into English for Perry Anderson's *The Antinomies of Antonio Gramsci*, 2017). 'We must,' Gramsci said, 'be more political, better able to act politically, less afraid of doing politics.' The fascists had strengthened their hold on the country and its institutions. Gramsci said that the Communists should give a call for the creation of a Constituent Assembly to 'pose the most urgent demands of the working class, to discredit every scheme for peaceful reform, and to show the Italian working class that the only viable solution for Italy lay in a proletarian revolution'. This, for Gramsci, was a 'period of transition'. The Communist Party, he said, 'could join forces with other parties fighting against fascism in Italy, but should not tail them'. The Party's final aim was for a socialist revolution, towards which end the Party had to build the independent strength and confidence of the working class, the peasantry, and other allied classes. Not for one minute did Gramsci lose faith in the revolutionary process, not for once did he abandon the idea of the proletariat as the leading force, and not once did he pause from offering his assessment of the conjuncture and the tactics required in that situation. He was a communist militant to the very end.

Gramsci in India

Gramsci describes the text of the *Prison Notebooks* as notes which he 'jotted down as quick prompts *pro memoria*. They are all to be punctiliously revised and checked, since they certainly contain imprecisions, false connections, anachronisms. Written without access to books to which they refer, it is possible that after checking, they should be radically corrected, as the very opposite of what they say proves true'. Till now, despite the fabulous work of Valentino Gerratana, Giuseppe Fiori, Perry Anderson, Joseph Buttigieg, and others, there is much to be revised about our thinking of Gramsci's fragmentary notes.

The first edition of Gramsci to appear in English was a section of the *Prison Notebooks* that had been translated by Louis Marks, a member of the Communist History Group with Eric Hobsbawm and Christopher Hill (*The Modern Prince and Other Writings*, Lawrence and Wishart, 1957). This volume was favourably reviewed by Bhabani Sen, a leader of the Communist Party of India, in *Parichay* (1957). Scattered references to Gramsci can be found in the writings of Indian academics and Indian communists, including the distinguished historian Susobhan Sarkar's 'Thought of Gramsci' in *Mainstream* (2 November 1968); Sarkar began to teach his students at Presidency College about Gramsci in this period.

A decade later, one of Sarkar's students – Ranajit Guha – used a term from Gramsci to anchor the Subaltern Studies collective, whose own engagement of Gramsci's considerable work was superficial. Special issues of *Indian Left Review* (1973), *Economic and Political Weekly* (1988), *Socialist Perspective* (1988), and *Society and Change* (1991–92) as well as conferences at the Joshi-Adhikari Institute of Social Studies in Kolkata (1991) and at the Nehru Memorial Museum and Library (1993) brought more of Gramsci's ideas into Indian political debate. Several books appeared on Gramsci by Ajit Ray, Sobhanlal Datta Gupta, Samik Bandyopadhyay, and Sourin Bhattacharya, while Aijaz Ahmad's 'Fascism and National Culture: Reading Gramsci in the Days of *Hindutva*', first delivered in Kolkata as the Amal Bhattacharji Memorial Lecture in 1992 and then published in *Social Scientist* (March–April 1993) attempted to elaborate Gramsci's concepts to make sense of the Indian conjuncture.

The context that spurred Aijaz Ahmad to interrogate Gramsci to understand the gallop of Hindutva across the Indian landscape also inspired EMS and P. Govinda Pillai to reflect on Gramsci's thought. Ahmad wrote of 'his world and ours', the conjuncture of Gramsci in the jaws of Italian fascism, and the conjuncture of India in the aftermath of the destruction of the Babri Masjid in Ayodhya on 6 December 1992. It is impossible to read *Gramsci's Thought* and not feel the hot breath of the RSS and the Bajrang Dal, of the men hacking away at a sixteenth-century mosque and of the millions of Indians fighting from the fields and the factories to advance their immediate demands against the brutalities of capitalism and of Hindutva.

This text is not a mere reflection on Gramsci or an attempt to understand Gramsci for an Indian context; *Gramsci's Thought* must be read as the attempt by two communists to recount the life and ideas of Gramsci as they attempted to understand their own time and develop the concepts to understand their present and to develop the tactics to advance the proletarian revolution. The *Prison Notebooks* is 'an exceptional tool', they write at the end of this book, to help the 'working class adopt the correct revolutionary position'.

At its heart is Gramsci's view that a communist is a person 'who takes sides, who is anchored to sound moral and political beliefs, does not conceal them, nor even tries'. The work of a communist, Gramsci wrote, is to 'struggle for culture, that is, for a new humanism, a critique of customs and feelings, a passionate fervour'. Such a project defines what EMS and P. Govinda Pillai champion in their book.

PART I

LIFE OF FULFILMENT

THE STORY OF GRAMSCI

AND HIS NOTES

'This brain should be prevented from functioning for the next two decades,' shrieked the prosecutor of Italy's Fascist regime at the conclusion of the trial of Antonio Gramsci, the general secretary of the Communist Party of Italy (*Partito Comunista d'Italia* – PCI) in 1926.

The court upheld this demand and sentenced Antonio Gramsci (1891–1937) to 20 years of imprisonment. However, much before the completion of Gramsci's incarceration, his health had seriously deteriorated leading to mounting international pressure on Italy's Fascist ruler Benito Mussolini (1883–1945) for his release. Though he was freed after ten years in prison, Gramsci's health had by then worsened beyond redemption and he passed away soon thereafter at the age of 46.

Even while languishing in prison, grappling with his extremely poor health, Gramsci had embarked on a mission to study and write comprehensively about politics and society. The notes he wrote in prison from 1926 to 1937, numbering 2,848 handwritten pages, were smuggled out through clandestine channels. These notes dwelt upon the various global challenges faced by Marxism-

Leninism, the working class as well as the specific issues related to Italy. These writings have turned out to be a treasure house of fresh ideas and insights on the theory and practice of Marxism.

Gramsci's notes from prison were published in a condensed form first in 1947 in Italy, ten years after his death, during the post-Second World War period. They soon caught the attention of Marxists and other scholars from all over the world who were awestruck to discover a gold mine. Even today, as the 20th century is passing into history, no one – Marxist or not – who writes on the diverse issues discussed by Gramsci, can advance without mentioning his works. Four years later, his collected works containing the *Prison Notebooks* and earlier writings were published in six major volumes in Italy.

Gramsci's political and social writings have been collected in two major volumes: *Pre-Prison Writings* and *Prison Notebooks*. Newer editions and interpretations of his works continue to come out even today in Italian as well as other European languages. The first short version of the *Prison Notebooks* in English was brought out in 1957 by Lawrence & Wishart of London. A longer version of the selected writings was published in 1971 by International Publishers in the USA. The key source for the present brief work is this edition, which contains notes, interpretations, and classification on a topical basis.* Many of Gramsci's works, biographies, interpretations and so on continue to come out in the English language.

Besides participating in the Italian revolutionary movement as one of the founder members of PCI, Gramsci had lived in Moscow

---

* The volumes of Gramsci's writings cited in the following pages are: *Selections from the Prison Notebooks of Antonio Gramsci*, ed. Quintin Hoare and Geoffrey Nowell Smith (New York: International Publishers, 1992); *Antonio Gramsci: Pre-Prison Writings*, ed. Richard Bellamy (Cambridge: Cambridge University Press, 1994); and *Selections from Political Writings, 1910–1920*, ed. Quintin Hoare (London: Lawrence & Wishart, 1977).—*Pub.*

and travelled extensively in other European countries as an office bearer of the Communist International. The *Prison Notebooks* contain the fruits of the rich experience as well as the critical and self-critical knowledge he gathered during this period.

Gramsci belongs to the league of international revolutionaries and Marxist thinkers like Rosa Luxemburg (1871–1919) and Mao Zedong (1893–1976), who made the most original and seminal contributions to the vast treasure house of the corpus of Marxist-Leninist knowledge after V.I. Lenin (1870–1924). Gramsci was able to re-invent the philosophy, politics and cultural positions of the proletariat as formulated by Karl Marx (1818–1883), Friedrich Engels (1820–1895), and Lenin. His interpretation was located within the matrix of the Italian revolution and has thus substantially enriched Marxist-Leninist studies and epistemology. It is impossible for contemporary Marxist-Leninists to proceed without imbibing Gramsci's *Prison Notebooks*.

A childhood in misery

In order to understand Gramsci, the working-class revolutionary and ideologue, it is imperative to know, at least briefly, of his life of extreme deprivation and sacrifice. The socio-political circumstances of his childhood had considerable influence on his evolution as a revolutionary.

Antonio Francesco Gramsci was born on 22 January 1921 in Sardinia, a Mediterranean island and southern province of Italy. Though part of Italy, the province was economically much poorer and backward compared to its northern provinces. Sardinia's history is filled with periodic invasions by various imperial powers, indigenous resistance movements against foreign domination, and revolts and struggles demanding secession from the mainland. Most of the land was owned by exploitative landlords belonging to the northern provinces. More discontent was sown among the local community by the Belgian-French capitalists who had converged in Sardinia to mine its precious metals. This 'Southern Question' was a thorny issue in Italian politics during Gramsci's time and later as well. Leaders of the Sardinian movement lamented that even the much-celebrated re-unification of Italy (*Risorgimento*), realized through the heroic struggles led by revolutionary nationalists Giuseppe Garibaldi (1807–1882) and Giuseppe Mazzini (1805–1872), had merely established Northern hegemony and Southern colonization.

Gramsci was born to a lower middle-class family in Ales, a Sardinian village caught in those turbulent times. Immediately after he was born, the family moved to Ghilarza in northern Sardinia. The fourth among seven siblings, Antonio went to primary school in Ghilarza and moved to the Sardinian port town of Cagliari for high school. During this time his father, Francesco Gramsci (1860–1937), a petty government official, was sent to prison on the charge that he had misused public funds. With the family's breadwinner in prison, Antonio had to discontinue his studies and find work to help his mother run the family. Later, Gramsci wrote about these days:

I started to go for work at the age of 11 in order to earn a living and run my family. I used to work 10 hours every day including Sundays. My daily wage of 8 lira enabled me to buy a kilogram of bread. My main job was to carry registers etc. which used to weigh more than me. During most nights I used to weep in the dark as my body ached unbearably.

Sick since his childhood, Antonio had also developed a hunch on his back on account of tuberculosis of the spine. No treatment was fruitful, and he became a lifelong hunchback. After his father was released from prison in 1904, Antonio could resume his studies again. Antonio went to school at Cagliari where he lived with his elder brother Gennaro Gramsci (1884–1965), who was a port worker. Gennaro was inclined towards socialism and deeply interested in the Sardinian struggles. The growing discontentment among people in Sardinia, Gennaro's socialist leanings, and the struggles of port workers significantly contributed to the bright young man's early political development. He used to proudly say later that Gennaro was his first political teacher.

Antonio, who was introduced to socialist writings and struggles in his school days, was a brilliant student. He received a government scholarship for academic excellence. This allowed him to join university.

Antonio left his beloved Sardinia in 1910 to join the University of Turin in the northern province of mainland Italy. Enrolled in the Department of Language and Literature in the university, he soon joined the Socialist Party (PSI) and, later, the Communist Party (PCI). Antonio became an office-bearer of the state party unit and subsequently moved to Moscow to work in the headquarters of the Communist International. Later, he returned to Italy to actively participate in the country's politics and went on to become the Opposition leader in the parliament. His life from the student days up to imprisonment in 1926 is an engaging narrative of the evolution of a globally renowned revolutionary. It is the story of the sixteen years that witnessed the maturing of his struggles, organizational efforts, and thoughts. It is also the story of the blossoming of a brain that Mussolini wanted to stop from functioning.

Chapter 2

EVOLUTION OF A REVOLUTIONARY

For Antonio, life in Turin was quite different from that in Sardinia. The 18-year-old villager from Italy's most backward region was stepping into the big, loud and vibrant world of an industrial city. Though burdened by many years of hard life, ill health, and a hunchback to boot, the village boy with a thirst for knowledge was immensely inspired by the university's academic potential as well as the workers' struggles that went on in the city.

Gramsci's teachers in the Language and Literature department included very eminent and well-known scholars and thinkers. Among them were the respected linguist Matteo Bartoli (1873–1946) and the great philosopher Benedetto Croce (1866–1952), names that remain highly popular even today. According to Gramsci's biographers, he had to struggle hard in order to free himself from the influences of these idealist thinkers, especially Croce, during his intellectual development towards embracing Marxism-Leninism. They all expected Gramsci to contribute much to the development of 20th century's linguistic sciences. Bartoli was too disappointed that his favourite student gave up a promising academic career, instead dedicating himself to full-time political activity. Among Gramsci's classmates was Palmiro Togliatti (1893–1964), who later became his staunch comrade and one of the tallest leaders of the PCI as well as the Communist International.

The inclination for struggle and also socialism that Gramsci imbibed from his Sardinian life and his brother had enabled him to closely involve himself with Turin's working-class movements. He gave up university studies to jump into full-time political activism even before the First World War broke out. In recognition of his pivotal role in organizing workers' anti-war struggles, Gramsci was elected as the secretary of the Socialist Party's town unit.

Like all revolutionaries in Europe, Gramsci was inspired by Lenin's call to oppose the World War and the bourgeois nationalist movements that supported it as well as to fight to transform the situation into civil strife leading to socialist revolution. Deeply entrenched in the works of Marx, Lenin and Engels, Gramsci became a confirmed Marxist with the triumph of the great October Revolution in 1917. The Marxist-Leninist stream inside the Italian Socialist Party soon began to emerge stronger.

The primary organization for working-class struggles in Italy during the period was the *factory council*. Gramsci believed that these councils ought to be developed to function as the soviets [in Russia] in the final revolutionary struggle. He launched *L'Ordine Nuovo* ('The New Order') as the mouthpiece of these councils in 1919 which carried most of the articles that he wrote until his arrest in 1926. Most of these articles appear in Gramsci's collected works named *Pre-Prison Writings*. Gramsci's articles in *L'Ordine Nuovo* help us understand the evolution of his thought as well as the application of Marxism-Leninism to Italy's national context. Mussolini banned the newspaper in 1923.

L'Ordine Nuovo had a key role in the gradual growth of the Italian working class's revolutionary movement and also in the birth of the Communist Party, which emerged out of the break-up of the Socialist Party at the Livorno Congress in January 1921. Gramsci – ahead of the other leaders of the Socialist Party – realized the significance of the political dimension of working-class struggles. Gramsci was in the editorial team of *Avanti!* ('Forward!'), which continues to be published and was then the mouthpiece of the Socialist Party. He wrote a column in that paper on theatre, and in these columns was one of the earliest critics to recognize the greatness of Luigi Pirandello (1867–1936) who went on to become one of the world's most acclaimed dramatists. Clearly, this demonstrates Gramsci's insight on art and culture even at such a young age. He was twenty-four years younger than Pirandello when he wrote the review. It may be noted that one of his earliest articles in *L'Ordine Nuovo* was on Leonardo da Vinci (1452–1519), the leader of the Italian Renaissance, painter and scientist. Even when *L'Ordine Nuovo* became the vanguard of Italian working-class politics, Gramsci used to describe it as an organ of proletarian culture. Like his *Prison Notebooks* later, his diverse articles in *L'Ordine Nuovo* indicate how Gramscian thought had imbibed a gamut of subjects ranging from politics and history to aesthetics, philosophy, and culture studies.

The Socialist Party under Filippo Turati (1857–1932) did not provide the space for Gramsci's comprehensive political perspective. The party was not prepared to take advantage of the favourable circumstances that emerged in the aftermath of the First World War and the October Revolution. This convinced Gramsci of the need for a new party and movement to be built on the basis of Marxism-Leninism. This led him to launch the new newspaper.

As mentioned earlier, *L'Ordine Nuovo* was planned as the mouthpiece of factory councils, which were transformed into revolutionary organizations during the war. The factory councils made full use of all the opportunities opened up by parliamentary politics; they explored the possibilities of agitations beyond the parliamentary sphere. The experience of the October Revolution confirmed Gramsci's positions. He wrote,

Is there any working-class tool in Italy which is comparable to the Soviets and has their characteristics? Any tool which would ensure that the Soviets are not merely a Russian organization or institution?

Gramsci argued that the factory council was the embryonic organization of the struggle which could carry the revolutionary potential of the working class. The activities and struggles of the factory councils led Gramsci and the cadres of his generation to come of age. Within five months after the launch of *L'Ordine Nuovo* in May 1919, factory councils went much beyond organizing workers' struggles; they began to think about how to plan and run industries. Factory owners were forced to recognize the powers of the councils. Much as their actions inspired the masses, the councils had also struck terror among the ruling classes. The retaliation began by the spring of 1919. The monarchy and the capitalists joined hands to destroy the councils and demolish their successes through all means. The period also marked the rise of Mussolini, a former leading member of the Socialist Party who emerged with his rudimentary fascist organization to fragment and hegemonize the working class. His organization, called the 'Black Shirts', was comprised of paid criminals and strike-breakers who unleashed violence in factories and on the streets against the agitating workers. The government and police embraced the Black Shirts as their ally.

A general strike was declared in 1922 to protect the councils, defend their achievements and protest against the repression by police and the Fascist thugs. Industrial workers of northern Italy were joined by peasants and agricultural workers of the south in the strike. The government, meanwhile, used Mussolini's hordes as a tool to repress the workers which in turn led to the digging of democracy's grave. The global imperialist media backed the tormentors by clamouring that Red Revolution was taking over

Italy. The brutal repression of the heroic struggle that lasted from 13 to 24 April was followed by a tragic era for Italy. The 'March on Rome' by Mussolini's 20,000 Black Shirts in late October 1922 laid the foundations for Fascism, which choked to death not only Italy's working-class movement but even the country's bourgeois democracy. On 30 October, Mussolini was invited by Italy's king Victor Emmanuel III (1869–1947) to form his Fascist government. Mussolini's dictatorship continued until the victorious anti-fascist guerrillas captured and hanged him on 28 April 1945 as the Second World War was coming to an end.

Gramsci and the Communist Party were not unaware of the Fascist danger when they had led the struggles under factory councils. In May 1920, Gramsci published an important document in *L'Ordine Nuovo*, which led to the formation of the Italian Communist Party in 1921. Captioned 'Towards a Renewal of the Socialist Party', the document was published by the Socialist Party of Turin. This document was praised by Lenin, who said its views were analogous to the principles and perspective of the Communist International. Demonstrating amazing foresight, Gramsci wrote,

The present phase in the class struggle in Italy is the phase that precedes *either* the conquest of political power on the part of the revolutionary proletariat and the transition to new modes of production that will allow a recovery in productivity; *or* a tremendous reaction on the part of the propertied class and the governing caste. No violence will be spared in subjecting the industrial and agricultural proletariat to servile work. There will be a bid to smash the working class's organs of political struggle (the Socialist Party) once and for all and to incorporate its organs of economic resistance (trade unions and co-operatives) into the machinery of the bourgeois State. (*Pre-Prison Writings*, p. 156)

Unfortunately for Italy and Europe, it was the second ominous possibility that came true. Failure to foresee this eventuality was the mistake of the Second Internationalists and Social Democrats in the Socialist Party. They complacently expected an inevitable progress to the socialist phase and failed to be vigilant of the fierce onset of fascism. The smug belief that fascism was just another errant bourgeois trend dissuaded them from formulating new political strategies and tactics. Even during those days, Gramsci had put forward the proposal to form a united front – even with bourgeois-democratic forces – to fight fascism. It was Gramsci who had pioneered the idea of a united front against fascism, which was later propounded as a strategy and tactic by the Communist International under its secretary general Georgi Dimitrov (1882–1949) of Bulgaria as well as Togliatti of Italy.

This political context convinced Gramsci and his comrades of the need to form a Marxist-Leninist party which would be free from all the deviations of the moderate Social Democracy. When the Communist Party of Italy (PCI) was launched in 1921 at the port city of Livorno, the programme adopted was the same document – with minor amendments – that had been written and published by Gramsci in *L'Ordine Nuovo* the previous year, and which had won Lenin's endorsement. Amadeo Bordiga (1889–1970) was elected the first secretary of the party.

Chapter 3

FRUITS OF AGONY

Gramsci could not rest even after the realization of his dream – for which he worked very hard – to form a Communist party. Even as the enemy outside began showing the fierce fangs of fascism, divisions grew within the communist movement over the organizational forms and agitations to be launched. Although these debates and techniques evolved over the experience of many struggles, Bordiga and other elder comrades were not convinced about the need for novel strategies to face new challenges. Gramsci's view was that even though fascism was a new political form for old capitalism, the old strategies and tactics would be insufficient to counter the barbarism of fascism. This view was accepted by the Communist International. Yet, Gramsci's view was dismissed as a timid surrender by Bordiga and other comrades. Apart from Bordiga and Gramsci, the PCI's top leadership consisted of Togliatti, Angelo Tasca (1892–1960), and Umberto Terracini (1895–1983).

Sick and weak from childhood, Gramsci's tuberculosis became worse owing to the hard work he had put in during the post-war period. However, his deputation to Moscow as Italy's representative to the Comintern enabled him to receive good medical care. Though Gramsci's activities were spread all over Europe while based in Moscow, he used to regularly address every issue faced by the PCI until 1926 when he returned to take over as its general secretary. His election to the post showed that the party recognized the value of his interventions.

During his time in Moscow, Gramsci had spent some days in a Russian sanatorium for treatment. Here he met Giulia Schucht (1896–1980), a young Russian violist. Agonized by the ascent of Fascism and his own ill health, Gramsci found solace in Giulia who attended to him with love and compassion. They got married in 1923 and had two sons – Delio (1924–1982) and Giuliano (1926–2007). When Gramsci was to return to Italy after the completion of his assignment in Moscow, Giulia was pregnant for the second time. But Gramsci was in prison by the time his second son was born, and he was not allowed to see Giulia or the newborn child. (Gramsci passed away before ever seeing the second son even once.) The repressive atmosphere in Italy was hardly suitable for the pregnant Giulia. After a few months spent in Vienna for work related to the Communist International, Gramsci arrived in a turbulent Italy in 1924.

This was Mussolini's heyday. Gramsci was elected as the new party secretary of the PCI. He won a seat to the Senate (parliament) as an Opposition candidate. Holding the election was Mussolini's attempt to provide a garb of legitimacy to his authoritarian rule. In spite of the misuse of state power and meddling by the Black Shirts, Communists and Socialists could emerge as an opposition with considerable mass support. Giacomo Matteotti (1885–1924), the Socialist leader who bravely challenged Mussolini's dictatorship in the parliament, was killed in the streets by the Black Shirts with the authorities' silent collusion. Political assassination and violence became routine against the Opposition which unanimously declared a boycott of the parliament. Mussolini hit back by suspending the parliament session indefinitely and threatened to disband it.

Within the ranks of the Opposition, Gramsci and the PCI argued that there was no other option than to go on the offensive against Mussolini's government. As a first step, Gramsci suggested that the Opposition call for a general strike. This suggestion was dismissed by the rest of the Opposition, including the Socialists. They foolishly believed that if they did not create any provocation, the King would intervene and dismiss Mussolini or at least rein him in. But the King chose to ignore all requests for intervention. In fact, he was too helpless to act.

With his confidence boosted by the Opposition's passivity, and to present a picture of peace and tranquillity, Mussolini reconvened the parliament. The Opposition continued the boycott of the parliament. Gramsci realized that there was not sufficient appetite for a general strike or other such actions; he, therefore, asked the Communist members to attend the parliament. The public was inspired by the impassioned speeches made by the Communists in the parliament against Mussolini's authoritarianism and against the violence unleashed by the Black Shirts in the streets and factories. Thus, Gramsci, who knew most about the futility of parliamentary institutions under fascism, utilized the parliament to break through the desert of passivity. Gramsci's two years of parliamentary action showed how much he had internalized Lenin's perspectives and tactics on the need to use the bourgeois parliament by utilizing and boycotting it as the occasion demanded.

Even as he was engrossed in the resistance against Fascism and despite his hectic schedule, Gramsci was deeply involved during this time in his studies on the strategy and tactics of the Italian revolution. His most important intellectual inquiry was on how to forge an alliance between the working class of Italy's industrialized north and the peasantry of the south. 'The Southern Question' was the name of the last article Gramsci wrote before he was imprisoned. This article was discovered later and published. It consists of original solutions to the Southern Question which had been a headache for political scientists, leaders, and governments ever since the days of Italian unification – known as the

Risorgimento ('Resurgence') – in the 19th century. Gramsci's article is a testimony to the creatively original way he applied Marxist-Leninist principles to Italian conditions.

In Mussolini's chambers and in imperialist boardrooms, vile conspiracies were being hatched against the Italian people. At the PCI's Third Congress, held in Lyons (France) in January 1926, the policies and strategy put forward by Gramsci and Togliatti received considerable support. While Gramsci and his comrades received 90.8 per cent of the votes by the delegates, former secretary Bordiga had to contend with just 9.2 per cent. The document Gramsci and Togliatti prepared for the Congress was named the 'Lyons Thesis'. This document is historic. The unanimity achieved inside the PCI on strategies and programmes and its elevation as the unofficial leader of the entire Opposition led to the eclipse of many of Mussolini's ambitions. His hopes to divide not just the Opposition but also the PCI went awry. Global attention turned to Italy.

The Fascist leadership realized it would be dangerous to wait any longer to strike. In the meanwhile, the sensational news flashed across that there was an attempt to assassinate Mussolini on 31 October 1926. It is not yet clear if the news was true or an exaggeration. Nevertheless, it provided the Fascists with the ruse they were waiting for to unleash repression.

On 5 November the government formulated certain emergency laws. They were passed by the parliament four days later. The objective of these laws was to put an end to bourgeois democracy in Italy. Following this the party made plans to move Gramsci to Switzerland. But he refused to leave Italy and resolved to participate in the debate on the emergency laws in parliament. Gramsci had believed that the differences within the ruling classes would help avert the danger to democracy. Later, Togliatti reported a more important reason for Gramsci's decision not to leave Italy: 'Antonio held that he could not leave Italy until the working class was convinced about its necessity and remaining here became absolutely impossible.' Gramsci himself wrote later from jail: 'The captain should be the last to escape from a sinking ship. He should remain until he is convinced that all the rest have escaped. Some believe that the captain should sink along with the ship. This is not a completely irrational view as it may appear.'

Gramsci's position is comparable to that of Ernst Thälmann (1886–1944), the German Communist Party's (KPD) general secretary, who also refused to follow his party's plans to move out of Hitler's Germany. Gramsci became terminally ill and died on account of his prison life; Thälmann was shot dead in jail on Hitler's orders. Thus became legendary the life and death of two illustrious leaders of the world Communist movement.

Gramsci's Russian wife Giulia was mentally shattered while he was in jail. Admitted to a hospital, she could not even correspond with her husband. Her elder sister Tatiana (1887–1943) came and stayed in Italy and helped in any way possible. Tatiana had managed to get a job in the Soviet Embassy at Rome. She was instrumental in bringing Gramsci's *Prison Notebooks* out of prison and also collecting his letters to his wife and sons.

These letters mark the humaneness of a revolutionary. The *Prison Notebooks* present the thoughts of a seasoned Communist. Both throw light on the great personality of Gramsci.

Chapter 4

FINAL DAYS

Even though the Fascist government proclaimed the Exceptional Laws for State Security on 9 November 1926, Gramsci was arrested a day before. A number of Communists – including Bordiga – Socialists, and Democrats were imprisoned in the days to come. But Togliatti who was in Moscow – the capital of the Communist International – escaped Mussolini's net.

Gramsci was captured in advance because the government feared he would go underground. Although he had no objection in principle to going underground, Gramsci thought it prudent in the given circumstances of Italy to work in the open. His reasons for this decision were discussed in the last chapter.

Considering Gramsci to be the most dangerous among the arrested, he was sent to solitary confinement to Ustica Island, located north of Sicily in southern Italy. A few weeks later, Gramsci was taken in a covered truck to Milan in northern Italy for his trial.

Though Gramsci arrived in Milan after an arduous journey in early 1927, he was not tried but sent to spend another year in an obscure prison. The trial of all leaders, including Gramsci, began in Rome in May 1928. Needless to say, the trial was a sham. Gramsci was sentenced to twenty years' imprisonment in order to 'stop his brain from functioning for the next two decades'. However, Mussolini miserably failed in this objective. Had Mussolini succeeded, we would not have received the great corpus of Gramsci's work which he created against unimaginable odds – both physical and mental – during his years in prison. Even this book – and many others in various languages from around the world after so many years – testifies to Mussolini's abject failure.

After a two-week journey, Gramsci was taken to a jail in Turi (Bari) in southern Italy. Louis Marks, who edited a collection of Gramsci's essays, wrote of the arduous journey:

> The journey from Rome to Turi during that unusually hot Italian summer was worse than a nightmare. He was carried in a truck used to transport cattle. As he was chained, Gramsci could neither stand nor lie down. The vehicle had to wait for hours or even days at rail crossings. That journey completely shattered the health of Gramsci who was already sick and handicapped. No medical attention was given to him though the authorities were informed of his worsening ailments before leaving Rome. During the journey, parts of his body got swollen and puss oozed from some of them. By the time he reached Turi, Gramsci was in a completely devastated state.

The nightmare continued. The authorities' intention was clearly to push Gramsci towards death. The poor food in prison and the absence of medical care tormented him. Even when his body was in a state of advancing decay, his determination and sense of purpose helped Gramsci keep his brain alert. The letters he wrote from prison bear witness to this purpose.

Gramsci could barely eat. He lost his teeth and his digestive system was in a poor state. Constant stomach ache, sleeplessness, and unending interrogations were too much to bear. Yet Gramsci did not lose his sense of humour even in these days of agony.

He wrote in a letter to his sister-in-law Tatiana Schucht on 4 November 1930:

> I have drawn up statistics for the month of October: only two nights did I sleep five hours, for nine whole nights I did not sleep at all, on the other nights I slept less than five hours in variable amounts which adds up to a general average of less than two hours per night. I myself wonder sometimes at having so much endurance and at not experiencing a general breakdown.

More than physical pain what saddened Gramsci most was the inability to meet his comrades and friends. Gramsci used to forget his physical ailments when he got involved in debates and discussions with them. As mentioned earlier, he could not even see his wife or children once he was imprisoned.

But neither his mental nor physical pain could defeat Gramsci's indomitable will or push him to self-pity or frustration. Even as he bore all the pain with a sagacious disinterest, he kept on writing and thinking in service of his life's mission – the revolution. Holding aloft his noble ideal, he wrote to his sister about his incarceration and agony with characteristic disdain:

> My incarceration is just one event in the great political struggle going on in Italy and the world. None can say how long this struggle would continue. My arrest is akin to nabbing an opponent during a war. I or others have joined the struggle fully aware of such or even worse consequences.

Even while strolling through the highest intellectual horizons, practical wisdom seldom left Gramsci. However, his practical wisdom never stooped to unethical compromises or opportunistic escapades. He once wrote about his practical wisdom to Tatiana:

> My practicality consists in this: in knowing that if you bang your head against the wall, it is your head that will crack and not the wall. This (knowledge) is my strength, my only strength.

Tormented by ailments throughout prison life, his condition became quite acute twice – in May 1931 and in March 1933. He nearly saw death before him on the second occasion. The news of his ailments broke through Mussolini's iron walls in various ways. Many prominent citizens from various European countries like Romain Rolland (1866–1944) in France and the Archbishop of Canterbury in England raised their voices on behalf of Gramsci's life. Appeals were made through newspapers and telegrams for reducing his prison term, giving him immediate medical care, and also releasing him. Finally, he was taken out of Turi prison to a clinic in Formia in Italy and subsequently to the Quisisana clinic in Rome after his condition became even worse. However, that precious life was in its final flicker. Convinced that his weak body was in its last pangs and that his brain would not function any more, Mussolini 'showed magnanimity' by reducing his prison term from 20 to 10 years. By then he had completed eleven years in prison. Barely a week after the announcement of his remission, Gramsci passed away on 27 April 1937.

Prominent Malayalam writer and film director K. Ravindran (1945–2011) thus summed up Gramsci's last journey and eventful life:

Antonio Gramsci breathed his last in a hospital in Rome at end of April 1937 at the age of 46. For ten years that life was rotting under severe mental and physical agony in Mussolini's prison. Through Roman streets – deserted on account of sudden heavy rains – his body was taken to the cemetery accompanied only by his brother Carlo and sister-in-law Tatiana. The funeral was conducted secretly under military vigil. Tatiana who was tending him in the last days managed to smuggle out notebooks numbering more than 30 amidst preparations for the funeral. These books, which Gramsci himself considered as providing an insight into his internal life and contained 2,848 cleanly handwritten pages, were later handed over by Tatiana to Togliatti, [the] Italian Communist Party's General Secretary. The fascist prosecutor had appealed to the Special Tribunal which tried Gramsci not to let his brain work for twenty years. As if on cue, the judge had sentenced him for 20 years. However, Gramsci could not sustain himself for the next 20 years. Yet the fascists could not stop his brain from working even for a minute. The famed *Prison Notebooks* and letters he penned in jail prove how his mind and intellect worked without rest even when he went through various serious ailments, enormous mental agony and unbearable physical conditions.

PART II

FOUNDATION STONES

Chapter 5

OLD WORDS, NEW MEANINGS

The vocabulary in use during a particular time in history is sufficient only for expressing the thoughts and discourses pertaining to that respective period. New ideas and thoughts would require new words for expression or that old words should find new meanings. Even creative literature is no exception to this, as pointed out by the illustrious Malayalam poet Kumaran Asan (1873–1924). Thus came into being new terms like 'Metaphysics' coined by Aristotle (384–322 BCE), 'Capitalism' by Marx or 'Agnosticism' by T.H. Huxley (1825–1895). Many old terms acquired new meanings in the course of time. 'Strike' came to mean agitation; 'train' became a vehicle with wagons linked together like a chain; 'journalism' meant media practice.

Gramsci who ventured into uncharted worlds of thought and expressed unprecedented ideas, had to invent new words to articulate them. Existing terms had to be bestowed with new meanings. The new words he coined turned out to be complicated because they were also intended to dupe the censors at his prison. It is difficult to comprehend Gramsci without acquiring a basic knowledge of the new terms he formulated. The following section is a cursory description of Gramscian terms.

Civil Society

This term appears frequently in Gramsci's writings. The meaning he gave to it was the body of *citizens*. 'Political society' is another term that frequently appeared in his writings by which he meant the State.

The term 'civil society' was used by Marx and Engels in their early writings as well as by their predecessors like John Locke (1632–1704), Jean-Jacques Rousseau (1712–1778), and Hegel (1770–1831). But the term does not appear much in the later writings of Marx and Engels. Locke, Rousseau, and Hegel used this term to describe the state of society after it came to be regulated by modern ways of governance and social rules as distinct from the pre-civilized societies governed only by the forces of nature.

But Marx used it with more exactitude to mean the bourgeois society that gradually replaced feudalism. 'Civil society' for him was the gradually emergent bourgeois society which was distinct from the State. People were divided into different social groups before the emergence of the bourgeois civil society which was based on equal status to every citizen both legally and formally. In the pre-bourgeois society, artisans belonged to their respective guilds while serfs and landlords to their respective Estates marked by hierarchy, or, like in India, where everyone was a member of a respective Caste. These diverse societies merged with each other to form the new civil society.

Marx had no doubt that, historically, the emergence of 'civil society' marked a step forward in human progress. But he never accepted this society's moral values or its libertarian pretensions. The replacement of traditional family ties and the feudal master-slave relationship by individual avarice for profit and unabashed pursuit of pleasure or the emergence of wealth as the only yardstick of happiness was not palatable to Marx's own values.

This basic Marxian approach – the dichotomy of *civil society* and *political society* – was also the basis of Gramsci's formulation. But Gramsci gave a much wider scope to the term 'civil society'.

Gramsci divided modern society into two levels. The first was the *civil society* that functioned and sustained itself on the basis of a general consent and mutual persuasion. Second was the *political society* or State, which functioned and sustained its power by the use of force. While the primary force that sustained political society was coercive power (courts, jails, police, army, punitive laws), civil society was nourished by leadership without the exercise of force but with consent and persuasion. Gramsci discussed the concepts of 'spontaneous' consent and mutual persuasion that sustain civil society within the matrix of the term 'hegemony'.

Hegemony

Like 'civil society', the term 'hegemony' too had been used by many including by Marxists. Traditionally, the domination of one country over another through physical force has been referred to as 'hegemony' in English dictionaries. Mao too used the term in this sense. Mao Zedong called what he saw as the Soviet Union's tendency to dominate as hegemonic ambitions. However, when we call for the need to establish the working class's hegemony over the nationalist movement, it is not similar to the domination imposed on one country by another. The term leadership too could hardly substitute for 'hegemony'. Although the term contains elements of leadership, hegemony indicates an internal supremacy driven by intellectual influence and persuasion. It is also different from the term 'hegemony' used by Mao to criticize Soviet policies. However, during the stage of socialist revolution, the working class should not just have hegemony, but it should directly hold leadership.

While the survival and strength of civil society depend upon ideological *hegemony*, political society is sustained by physical force and violence. According to Marxist analysis, the State is formed by a class or a class-alliance which imposes its authority over another class or class-alliance through the use of force. But Gramsci points out that though force is the basis of the State, it is secured and sustained only through the ruling class's ideological hegemony over civil society. Hence, to destroy the State and capture power, the ascending class has to establish hegemony over civil society.

Gramsci takes forward Lenin's teaching, expounded in works like *What Is To Be Done?* (1902), that the socialist consciousness would be realized only when workers go beyond trade unionist concerns regarding economic interests and imbibe the realization of the need for waging deeper political struggle. Only such consciousness would lead to the formation of true Communist revolutionaries. Gramsci's thoughts underscore the decisive significance of theory and praxis, socialist education, and cultural reformation in revolutionary activities and for waging class war. He delineates in detail the ways to put these ideas to practice. According to Gramsci, ideology is the tool to establish working-class hegemony over civil society.

Much as hegemony over civil society and violence are indispensable to sustain the State or political society, the revolutionary class's ideological hegemony and violence are essential to challenge the State. The relevance of violence in revolutionary struggle as well as its chances of victory hinge upon the revolutionary class's success in establishing its hegemony over civil society.

As long as the ruling class has its hegemony over civil society, it will grant it democratic freedoms and follow democratic procedures. The moment its hegemony ends or wanes, the State will move towards authoritarianism, strengthening its elements of violence and repression. Hence the point that fascism suffers from gross internal weaknesses in spite of its pretensions of power and authority. Capitalism moves towards fascism or authoritarianism in the name of *emergency* when it falls into a deep and irreparable crisis or when it is overwhelmed by the fear of an imminent end. Gramsci's findings in this topic enrich Marxism-Leninism without moving away from the fundamentals.

Ideology

The term 'ideology' crops up often in the discussions about hegemony. This term is highly complex and assumes even diverse and contradictory connotations in different contexts.

Although the concept of ideology was vital to Gramsci, he did not have to find new meanings for the term, for it already had wide and diverse dimensions. All he did was to pick the dimension he wanted in order to espouse his argument. Terry Eagleton, the well-known contemporary English Marxist philosopher and aesthetician, has given sixteen different meanings to the term 'ideology'. Some of them are not only mutually incompatible but even contradictory.

'Ideology' literally connotes a corpus of ideas. However, this definition is not sufficient to understand even a minor aspect of this unique term's meaning. Below is the definition of ideology given in a dictionary of philosophy published in the former Soviet Union:

A scheme that comprises of political, legal, moral, aesthetic, religious, and philosophical perspectives and ideas. The ideology which is part of the superstructure and that mirrors the society's economic relations. Ideological struggle reflects class war in a society where classes exist with mutually conflicting interests. Ideology can reflect reality rightly or wrongly, scientifically or otherwise.

In one of Marx and Engels's early (but unpublished) works – *The German Ideology* (1846) – 'ideology' was mentioned only as 'false consciousness' which reflected reality upside down.

When the aforementioned dictionary cites Marxism-Leninism as an example of the right ideology, it is meant as a theoretical apparatus as well as a plan of action. It then comes up to the level of philosophy which is subject to scientific inquiry and analysis by reason. However, ideology consists of many elements related to habits, subjective preferences, rituals, beliefs, and faith which need not subscribe to reason or scientific examination. Otherwise, how could ideology mirror not just true but even 'false consciousness'? Besides the consciously imbibed ideas, ideology also contains tastes and preferences that exist in the unconscious.

In the next chapter we examine how Gramsci used this term, fraught with so many contradictions and complexities.

Chapter 6

GRAMSCI'S IDEOLOGY

In Marx and Engels's works of the 1840s, ideology is referred to as 'false consciousness' or as a perception that stands reality on its head. The concept of false consciousness refers to the systematic misrepresentation of dominant social relations in the consciousness of subordinate classes that conceal or obscure the realities of their own state of subordination or exploitation. These founders of scientific socialism were using the prevailing terminology in order to combat the dominant thought of Georg Wilhelm Friedrich Hegel and Ludwig Feuerbach (1804–1872) and also the theological perspectives of the Bauer brothers – Bruno (1809–1882) and Edgar Bauer (1820–1886). While Hegel saw the ultimate realization of the idea of the Absolute (of the Ideal too) in the authoritarian Prussian monarchy of the day, Marx found this an ideological perspective which masked that government's class character and true class history. It was when Hegel's dialectics led him to such a conclusion that Marx famously said he was turning Hegel on his head! This was the reason 'ideology' received a negative connotation in the writings of Marx and Engels (*German Ideology, The Holy Family*) during that period. By the time they came to write the *Communist Manifesto* (1848), even though the old meaning did not undergo a total transformation, the change in emphasis was evident. The following reference in the *Manifesto* throws light not just on the meaning of ideology but on its role in social development and structure as well:

> The charges against Communism made from a religious, philosophical and, generally, from an ideological standpoint, are not deserving of serious examination.

Here one may be prompted to see the reference to ideology as purely counter-revolutionary. Besides, revolutionary ideas are referred to only as 'ideas' and not 'ideology'. The *Manifesto* continues:

> Does it require deep intuition to comprehend that man's ideas, views, and conception, in one word, man's consciousness, changes with every change in the conditions of his material existence, in his social relations and in his social life?
>
> What else does the history of ideas prove, than that intellectual production changes its character in proportion as material production is changed? The ruling ideas of each age have ever been the ideas of its ruling class.
>
> When people speak of the ideas that revolutionize society, they do but express that fact that within the old society the elements of a new one have been created, and that the dissolution of the old ideas keeps even pace with the dissolution of the old conditions of existence. (Chapter II, 'Proletarians and Communists')

Here the authors not only explain the role of ideas in social progress but also explain their epistemological roots and sources. Initially, ideology was referred to as the search related to the origin and development of ideas and their analysis. Subsequently, the term came to be applied to the paradigm of specific ideas, beliefs, and plan of action. Thus, ideology is simultaneously the content as well as the knowledge about it. Gramsci writes about this evolution of meaning:

> How the concept of Ideology passed from meaning 'science of ideas' and 'analysis of the origin of ideas' to meaning a specific 'system of ideas' needs to be examined historically. In purely logical terms the process is easy to grasp and understand. (*Prison Notebooks*, p. 376)

From a historical point of view, it could be said that the discovery which left a deep impact on the origin of ideas came about in 18th-century France. This marks the dawn of Enlightenment, with its epicentre in France, which swept across Western Europe. According to the philosophy of the Enlightenment all knowledge and ideas have emerged only from the empirical world, that is from the experience of the five senses of sight, hearing, touch, smell, and taste. Nothing was knowable from beyond these five senses. It was certainly a leap forward from the tradition of placing all knowledge and ideas at the feet of God, soul or a *sui generis* fruit of an exceptional human brain. Yet, this fell behind the subsequent Marxist postulation that all ideas take birth from human activity or praxis which in turn fuel thinking processes leading to the formation of knowledge (Mao, *On Practice*, 1937).

Gramsci pointed out that not just Sigmund Freud or Benedetto Croce had failed to comprehend this progress in understanding but even Marxists like Nikolai Bukharin (1888–1938) had failed. He subjected Bukharin's well-known 1921 work, *Historical Materialism: A System of Sociology* (written as a primer on Marxism for the masses), to criticism:

> One should examine the way in which the author of the *Popular Manual* has remained trapped in Ideology; whereas

the philosophy of praxis represents a distinct advance and historically is precisely in opposition to Ideology. Indeed, the meaning which the term 'ideology' has assumed in Marxist philosophy implicitly contains a negative value judgment and excludes the possibility that for its founders the origin of ideas should be sought for in sensations, and therefore, in the last analysis, in physiology. 'Ideology' itself must be analysed historically, in terms of the philosophy of praxis, as a superstructure. (*Prison Notebooks*, p. 376)

Thus, Gramsci brings his ideological conception into the classical Marxist framework. Marx had used the architectural concepts of 'base' and 'superstructure' to explain the relationship between forces of production and the world of ideas which are respectively described as the base and superstructure. Even as he used this conceptual framework, Marx had never denied the superstructure's independent laws of dynamics or its autonomous existence. Marx sees that even though the superstructure stands atop the base, the former could influence, accelerate or decelerate the latter's growth and development on occasion in varying degrees. This superstructure does not conform only to the clearly defined definitions, but is also influenced by emotions, habits, beliefs, and aspirations. Gramsci points out in the above quote that ideology belongs to or constitutes the major part of the superstructure.

Here Gramsci attracts our attention to another point. Why do we quarrel over an ideology if it is an inevitable outgrowth from a clearly defined base? We certainly have to quarrel. For 'there could be error in judging the right and wrong of an ideology', writes Gramsci.

There are two things that emerge in the name of ideology. First, ideology is seen as an expression or reflection of the social structure or its elements. Second, ideology is understood as false consciousness or as an arbitrary expression of an individual or a group which does not represent the social structure. The latter is willed and rationalized but not genuine or natural. The former is legitimate, but the latter is not. Illegitimate ideology hinders progress and change, while legitimate ideology is in tune with natural evolution. Gramsci puts forward yet another concept – the 'historically organic ideology'. This is necessary for the smooth and natural advancement of the social structure or its elements. Gramsci refers to the proponents and practitioners of organic ideology as *Organic Intellectuals*. Those who are in the opposite camp are called *Traditional Intellectuals*. This is discussed in detail in the next chapter.

Gramsci focuses on what Marx called the 'solidity of popular beliefs'. What he indicates is Marx's proposition that ideas and theories become a material force when they are imbibed by the masses. Says Gramsci,

The analysis of these propositions tends, I think, to reinforce the conception of *historical bloc* in which precisely material forces are the content and ideologies are the form, though this distinction between form and content has purely didactic value, since the material forces would be inconceivable historically without form and the ideologies would be individual fancies without the material forces. (*Prison Notebooks*, p. 377)

While creatively analysing ideology, Gramsci thus defines its function:

To the extent that ideologies are historically necessary they have a validity which is 'psychological'; they 'organise' human masses, and create the terrain on which men move, acquire consciousness of their position, struggle, etc. (Ibid.)

According to Gramsci, illegitimate ideology too has a utilitarian function like legitimate ideology. It is akin to the value of a wrong when it helps one to compare and understand the value of good.

56

Chapter 7

PHILOSOPHY OF PRAXIS

Gramscian thought is remarkable for its encyclopaedic sweep and diversity. It has – as its undercurrent – a comprehensive vision. Gramsci called this vision the 'philosophy of praxis'. It is in no way contrary to or fundamentally different from Marxist philosophy. But Gramsci gives certain ideas much sharper and fuller focus particularly in the context of European, especially Italian, thought of the day. It is quite appropriate since the philosophical perspective and political content that animate Marxism too are in the constant process of evolution and growth. Everything that stays alive has to keep growing. The moment the process of growth ends, it is dead for ever. Like Lenin or Mao, Gramsci has thus helped Marxian philosophy grow with time.

In order to comprehend the essence of Gramsci's thought it is important to have a general understanding of Italy's philosophical-cultural tradition as well as the philosophical milieu in which he was born and brought up. Only this would help one see the various legacies of thought that Gramsci contested or imbibed in order in order to arrive at his idea of *praxis*.

The Renaissance – which grew from the roots of Roman culture – enabled the great developments of European history. Roman civilization and culture bloomed in the years that immediately preceded and followed the advent of the Christian era. It marked a continuity with, and an echo of, Greek culture. Greek civilization, which was eclipsed after it bequeathed its great legacy to the world, could not regain its glory. Roman civilization, on the other hand, was not destroyed by the Christianization of the 4th century, by the relocation of Rome's centre to Byzantium on the Black Sea, and by the dark shadow of the Middle Ages. It flourished again from the 13th century with the Italian Renaissance led by Dante (1265–1321), Petrarch (1304–1374), Leonardo da Vinci (1452–1519), Michelangelo (1475–1564), and others. This Renaissance impacted not only Europe, but also the rest of the world.

The modern world is certainly a product of the European Renaissance, triggered by Italy. Thanks to Rome, which has always been the headquarters of the Catholic Church – the bulwark of global orthodoxy – Italy always remained the hub of global politics and the arena for contesting streams of thought. Among the brave intellectual warriors in this arena were also those who became targets of the Vatican's ire, such as Giordano Bruno (1548–1600) and Galileo Galilei (1564–1642).

The tradition of conflicts and evolution set off by the Renaissance continued to shake Italy even in the 19th century, when Gramsci was born. Italian society remained dominated during this age by legends like Mazzini, Garibaldi and Camillo Benso (1810–1861), who had fought with arms and ideas to liberate and unify a fragmented Italy from its subjugation to the Austro-Hungarian empire. Arts, literature, and philosophy in Italy witnessed new initiatives which either preceded this political and social revolution or were its consequence. Echoes of changing times began to be heard even inside the Catholic Church, conventionally a veritable enemy of change.

All these churnings shook Italy. Yet, the boy from the backward and isolated Sardinia was not quite aware of these developments. While the exploitation and poverty suffered by Sardinians and their resistance against them had made Gramsci a rebel, his life with his brother Gennaro confirmed his socialist beliefs. However, these had not made him go beyond being discontented with the system. Before Gramsci arrived at Turin University armed with a government scholarship, universal horizons of knowledge and action had opened up in Italy.

While the atmosphere in the university was shaken by the cerebral waves triggered by ingenious professors like Bartoli, de Sanctis, and Croce, the industrial city bustled with its militant working class. In neighbouring France, August Comte's (1798–1857) Positivist philosophy and humanist thoughts – propounded by writers like Romain Rolland – were making waves. Standing out from this flood of diverse thoughts was a clear and sparkling stream: Marxism. The Socialist Party (the name Socialist was adopted in 1893), which was formed during Engels's time, had paved the way for Marxism to flow ahead. Professor Antonio Labriola (1843–1904) of the University of Rome is considered the first spokesperson and interpreter of Italian Marxism.

The early proponents of the modern thought that led Italy towards Marxism included persons like the political philosophers Niccolò Machiavelli (1469–1527) of Florence, who lived during the height of the Renaissance, and Giambattista Vico (1668–1744) of Naples. It is not surprising that names such as Comte, Croce, Vico and Machiavelli are frequently mentioned in Gramsci's writings. Gramsci's intellectual and political evolution occurred during the time when various forms of thought such as Maximalism, Syndicalism, Positivism, and Jacobinism – some attached to these philosophers – were exerting deep influence on the socialists. Some of them were influenced by socialism, some were opposed to it, and others simply pretended to be socialists.

Gramsci also came under the influence of some of these theories during his intellectual evolution. When his experiences and his studies led him ultimately to Marxism, Gramsci had to sever some of these older cerebral links – sometimes openly clashing with them and settling scores with them. This is what makes Gramsci's Marxism a critical and attentive assessment of the traditions of Italian thought. Gramscian thought marks the creative intersection between Italian historical experiences and theories and the universal truth in Marxism-Leninism.

Hegel, Marx, Labriola

The post-Renaissance progress of European traditional thought continued in Italy, Germany, France, and England to different degrees. According to Marxist historians, the epitome of this classical philosophical tradition could be found in the German thinkers Georg Wilhelm Friedrich Hegel and Ludwig Feuerbach. The roots of dialectics in Marxism could be found in Hegelian thought, while its materialism could be traced to Feuerbach.

Hegel was a philosopher who exerted a major influence on European intellectuals of the 19th century. Like Marx and Engels, Antonio Labriola too had come under Hegel's influence. Later, based on a perspective shaped by Marx and Engels, Labriola too had distanced himself from Hegel.

Labriola made his own contribution to point out the role of action in the growth of the philosophical perspective. This was taken further by Gramsci which led him to the formulation of the idea of the 'philosophy of praxis'. Gramsci borrowed this term from Labriola. In the *Prison Notebooks*, Gramsci used this phrase to refer to the philosophy of Marx and Engels. 'Praxis' is a term with its origin in the Greek language and has a deeper philosophical meaning than the term 'practice'. Practice which invokes social responses or has a social objective is *praxis*. It is said that there was another reason why Gramsci used this term (which he revealed on certain occasions): had Gramsci directly mentioned the philosophy of Marx and Engels, the authorities might have objected. Hence, the use of the new term was only to dupe them.

But there was an even more fundamental reason. The very being of the philosophy of Marx and Engels was linked to the growth of the democratic movement led by the proletariat. However essential remains the role of ideas, practical action is equally important.

As Marx said famously, 'philosophers have hitherto only *interpreted* the world in various ways; the point is to *change* it' (*Theses on Feuerbach*, 1845). Marx has also written elsewhere, 'As philosophy finds its material weapon in the proletariat, so the proletariat finds its spiritual weapon in philosophy' (*A Contribution to the Critique of Hegel's Philosophy of Right*, 1844).

Based on these Marxist ideas, the young Gramsci found it obligatory for working-class revolutionaries to equally reject philosophy that was divorced from action as well as action which had no philosophical content. Gramsci was profoundly influenced by Marx's concept that, when they grip the imagination of the masses, ideas become a material force in and of themselves.

This vision is visible throughout Gramsci's *Prison Notebooks*. What had prompted Gramsci to write it was the bourgeois reactionary trend which had begun to grow in the capitalist world, particularly in his own country, assuming its concrete form in Benito Mussolini's Italian fascism.

Gramsci had embarked on the examination of the social, cultural, and political issues faced by the world and Italy in this context. In this endeavour he had to stress the fact that Marxism-Leninism was a philosophy of praxis. When he was attracted to the Italian socialist movement, Gramsci used to be a critical follower of Labriola on the intellectual level. At that time, he was only an admirer of the Italian socialist movement. However, the term – 'philosophy of praxis' – formed a significant landmark in Gramsci's growth from Italian socialism to international communism.

Philosophy for Gramsci was not just a tool to analyse complex issues or to find solutions. Praxis was ingrained in his thought and life. He explained how praxis – a social action with a clear objective – helps negotiate hurdles, even when faced with setbacks and failures. In the background of the collapse of the Factory Council movement of 1919–20, Gramsci wrote in *L'Ordine Nuovo*,

> It would be ridiculous to whine about what has happened and what is irremediable. Communists are cold and calm reasoners – they have to be. If everything lies in ruins, then everything has to be done again. The Party has to be rebuilt, and henceforth the communist fraction must be considered and esteemed as a party in its own right, as the solid framework of the Italian Communist Party. It must form disciples, organize them on a solid basis, educate them and turn them into the active cells of a new organism, that is developing and will develop until it becomes the whole of the working class, until it becomes the soul and will of the whole of the working people. (*Political Writings, 1910–1920*, p. 364)

It was the strength of Gramsci's philosophy that formed the basis of his optimism even when all lights were going out and darkness was spreading, with death staring him in the face.

Chapter 8

OCTOBER REVOLUTION

AND ANTI-FASCIST STRATEGY

The First World War (1914–18) is said to have opened a new age in human history because it led to the transition from capitalism to socialism thanks to the revolution of October 1917. It was the bourgeois-democratic revolution in Russia that brought the authoritarian tsarist empire to an end in February (March according to the new calendar) that had paved the way for the socialist revolution six months later (7 November according to the new calendar).

Differences had surfaced among various Socialist and Labour parties of the day on many key issues such as the events that led to the First Word War, the positions to be held by working-class parties of different countries regarding war, and the assessment of the revolutions of February and October. These differences had led to the collapse of Second International dominated by moderates and defectors and its eventual replacement by the Third International established under Lenin's leadership in 1919. The positions Gramsci had taken on many of these controversial issues based on his own analysis, enriched by Leninist thought, made him the person we all know and admire. It was a time when even people like Plekhanov or Kautsky, who prided themselves on having learnt Marxism directly from Engels, went wayward.

Influence of the Russian Revolution

On 29 April 1917, Gramsci wrote in the Italian Socialist Party's mouthpiece on Russia's bourgeois revolution of February,

> The bourgeois newspapers have stressed the question of power, telling us that the forces of autocracy have been replaced by other forces, whose identity is as yet uncertain, but which they hope will prove to be the forces of the bourgeoisie. And they have immediately established a parallel between the Russian revolution and the French Revolution, and they have found the events to be similar. But it is only on the surface that they resemble each other, as one act of violence resembles another act of violence and one act of destruction another. And yet I am convinced that the Russian Revolution is an act of proletarian spirit, as well as a historical event, and that it will necessarily result in a socialist regime. (*Pre-Prison Writings*, pp. 31–2)

These views were quite similar to the ideas expressed in Lenin's famed *April Theses*. As the French Revolution earlier, the Russian Revolution of February too was bourgeois in its class character. Yet both Lenin and Gramsci said it would inevitably lead to a socialist revolution. This marked a turning point in Gramsci's political evolution.

The Russian Revolution's influence had spread all through the Italian Socialist Party. By the time the socialist revolution occurred in Russia followed by the formation of the Third International in 1919, the entire Italian Socialist Party – cutting across the Right, Left or middle factions – joined as a member of the International.

This change in perspective was imbided by the Italian Socialist

Party. Gramsci comprehended the essence of the change in perspective more than anyone, for the following reasons:

1. Unlike most of the right-wing socialists, Gramsci could understand the theories of Marx and Engels as the philosophy for practical action.
2. Gramsci could elevate the alliance between the industrial working class-dominated northern Italy and the peasantry-dominated south as a larger front of workers and peasants.
3. Even when Russia witnessed the February revolution, Gramsci could foresee that it would overcome its own bourgeois limitations and lead to the socialist revolution.

Internal struggle

These circumstances led to the beginnings of the formation of a sharply Communist group inside the Italian Socialist Party. However, even within this group there were sections influenced by 'Left-Wing Communism' – called an 'infantile disorder' by Lenin. Among them were many who had come in for severe criticism by Lenin during the Second Congress (1920) of the Communist International.

There were many who had taken the left-wing position to boycott all bourgeois parliamentary institutions including elections. Even Gramsci felt the impact of these views. There was also a Right wing which had uncritically accepted bourgeois parliamentarism in the name of making use of parliamentary institutions and elections. Amadeo Bordiga of the Left wing was the most popular leader among the Italian Communists, while Angelo Tasca led the Right wing.

Both these lines had to be fought and defeated in order to follow the Leninist principle of radically using bourgeois parliamentary institutions for strengthening the working-class movement. Only thus could the Italian Communist Party be developed into a Bolshevik party.

Following this approach of the Communist International, Gramsci played a crucial role in the simultaneous struggles within the party against both the Left and Right. This struggle led to Gramsci replacing Bordiga, who was the Italian Communist Party's first general secretary. Gramsci was joined in this mission by many prominent leaders of the party including his college mate, Togliatti.

Opposition to Fascism

The Italian Communist Party had to settle a major political issue even before Gramsci assumed office. The cascading revolutionary upsurge following the revolution was effectively blocked in Russia. Rightist reactionary forces, with vehement opposition to communism as their hallmark, were surging ahead across Europe. As part of this, Benito Mussolini, a former Socialist leader of Italy had founded a fascist party. His party organized a series of physical attacks with the support of the bourgeois government against the Leftists in general and Communists in particular. Many views came up in the Communist Party as to how to counter these attacks.

A section of left-wing Communists led by Bordiga, the general secretary, held that fascism was just another facet of bourgeois rule. They argued that it was the dictatorship of the proletariat which should come into force after defeating fascism. They could not even imagine the resurrection of bourgeois democracy during the period between the defeat of fascism and the emergence of proletarian dictatorship.

Gramsci firmly opposed this inside the party. He argued that a bourgeois-democratic set-up could be resurrected with the participation of Socialists in which Communists too should play a creative role. He pointed out the need for such a stage to prepare the ground for the proletariat's final ascent. Although the Right wing led by Tasca too was of this opinion, Gramsci had differed with them on certain fundamental issues. Gramsci held that the factory workers' councils should be the main link in the broad anti-fascist alliance which would have Socialists and other democrats in its fold. According to him the 'soviet system' had to be adapted in Italy in the form of factory councils and other fighting organizations of the working class.

Gramsci believed that the masses – organized and fighting – should be the heart and soul of the anti-fascist alliance. The alliance of Socialists and other democratic forces would be their allies. Thus, Gramsci came to a position from where he could formulate strategies and tactics that opposed Left sectarianism on the one hand, as well as Right opportunism on the other. This political position eventually led to the adoption of the strategy of forming a broad anti-fascist alliance at the Seventh Congress of the Communist International a decade later.

It was the general secretary of the Soviet Communist Party (CPSU), Georgi Dimitrov, who had presented the all-important report at the Seventh Comintern Congress (1935). The report was a much higher and elaborate version of the tactical line Gramsci had begun to implement in the Italian party.

The Italian party's Togliatti had presented a supplementary report at the Congress. It had the indelible mark of the experiences and anti-fascist strategies of Gramsci and his comrades. The report had stressed the possibility of the Second World War breaking out, ways to avert it and, in case they fail, the ways to face the fascist upsurge including the need to formulate an international anti-fascist front with representation of the bourgeois governments opposed to fascist powers.

Togliatti had pointed out the possibility of the war beginning with the outbreak of mutual conflicts between imperialist forces only to end up soon as an anti-Soviet onslaught. As he foresaw, the Second World War, which broke out initially with skirmishes amongst the imperialist forces, soon became a battle to protect the USSR as well as all other states that sought to protect their national sovereignty.

Gramsci was in prison when the Seventh Congress of the International took place. But the revolutionary war tactics adopted at the Congress were first formulated by Gramsci in the Italian party. Thus, Gramsci arose as a leader who left an indelible mark in the history of the world Communist movement.

Ideological struggle

Intense debates were on inside the Soviet Communist Party and the Communist International at the time when Gramsci was elevated as the Italian Communist Party's secretary. Many warring groups, all claiming to be the true successors of Lenin, had emerged in the leadership of both the Soviet party as well as the International. Trotsky's group strongly opposed the dominant group led by Stalin and Bukharin. The Soviet party leadership decided to initiate action against Trotsky and his group. Although Gramsci supported this, he wrote a letter to the CPSU Central Committee expressing alarm at the way things were moving inside the movement.

'Unity and discipline should not be mechanical or forced. They must arise from loyalty and conviction,' he wrote. He reminded the CPSU Central Committee that action to implement discipline against those who falter should not prompt them to think of how to escape or hit back. Gramsci in another letter stressed the importance of the 'Leninist approach' in bringing unity, which was not superfluous but deeply rooted within the party. In the same letter Gramsci also expressed suspicion about the Bolshevik party's capability to bring about such a unity.

Days after he wrote this letter, Gramsci was arrested. Hence, he did not get an opportunity to express his opinion or comment on the debates and differences inside the Soviet party or inside the International. But it was amply clear from his brief comments that Gramsci was deeply disturbed by the developments in the CPSU and the International. Unfortunately, later developments in both the CPSU and the International proved that his fears were more than justified.

The strong criticism of Stalin at the CPSU's Twentieth Congress (1956) had marked a major stage during those developments. Much of that critique was accepted by Marxist-Leninists all over the world. However, Gramsci's successor Togliatti's opinion about that critique assumes special significance. Along with Stalin's remarkable achievements, unacceptable mistakes too had occurred during his tenure. Togliatti pointed out that the Soviet leadership had failed to examine the reasons for the mistakes with honesty and objectivity. Togliatti called for a self-critical re-assessment of the attempts to create a socialist society in the Soviet Union. That has not been done yet. The Communist Party of India (Marxist)'s Fourteenth Congress (1992) pointed out and reiterated this fact. Why did the Soviet Union face such a huge setback even after seven decades of existence? An incisive examination into its reasons remains highly warranted.

Gramsci had pointed out its key reason before he passed away. Attempts to bring about unity and discipline in the Party should be realistic and deliberate instead of being mechanical and forcible. But history proved that the unity and discipline brought about by Stalin and his successors were not of that nature.

However, in the name of correcting Stalin's mistakes, another tendency also appeared later – the abandonment of even the basic tenets of creating a socialist society. This led to the collapse of the Soviet Union and the East European Socialist nations. This was openly pointed out by the CPI (M) and by other Marxist-

Leninist parties of the world. What is important is that even while incarcerated in the fascist prison that imposed serious restrictions on the flow of information, Gramsci had the insight to foresee the fundamental flaws of the Soviet Socialist model that eventually led to disastrous consequences.

PART III

THEMES

Chapter 9

THE INTELLECTUALS

Gramsci begins his *Prison Notebooks* with a chapter titled 'The Intellectuals'. (Most titles and chapter divisions were done later by editors.) While those who do physical labour are called labourers, those who put in intellectual or mental labour are called 'intellectuals'. But the 'intellectual' mentioned by Gramsci has a much larger role and function. As Marx pointed out, the ideas that dominate a society are those of the class which dominates it. 'The ideas of the ruling class are in every epoch the ruling ideas, i.e. the class which is the ruling material force of society, is at the same time its ruling intellectual force' (*The German Ideology*).

The ideas that ruled during the periods of slavery or feudalism in the world or under the upper caste-landlord-feudal system in India were those of the slave owners, feudal lords or the upper-caste landlords.

However, even as a class society's predominant ideas are those of the ruling classes, those of the subaltern classes also get gradually formed during the period. As in the social, economic, and political spheres, classes clash with each other in the realm of ideas too. Hence, Engels and Lenin pointed out that in order to rise as an independent class, the working class should emerge dominant not only in the economic and social spheres but the world of ideas as well. The basis of the Leninist concept of a revolutionary party for the working class is the need to wage class war in the economic-political-theoretical realms under a centralized leadership. Gramsci's effort here is to develop this Leninist concept on the basis of the experiences of the Italian revolutionary movement.

A major issue that arose in the theoretical struggle inside the Italian Socialist Party was related to the idea of 'socialist culture'. Gramsci led the efforts to organize cultural activities because he knew that unless they took steps to build a culture of the proletariat simultaneously with organizing militant trade unions, the working class would not be able to emerge as a revolutionary force. Gramsci's efforts attracted praise from Lenin. All this had provided the backdrop for Gramsci writing on 'The Intellectuals' from his prison cell.

Intellectuals – representatives of a class

Gramsci began the chapter with the following question: 'Are intellectuals an autonomous and independent social group, or does every social group have its own particular specialized category of intellectuals?' (*Prison Notebooks*, p. 5)

According to Gramsci, this was a complex question. For the historical processes which produce intellectuals of different classes are diverse. Gramsci said two points have to be noted when examining this diversity. Firstly, each social group produces one or more types of intellectuals in relation to its different stages of growth. These intellectuals provide the group with its identity and unity. Each social group comes to understand its role in the social and political spheres through its own intellectuals. For instance, the entrepreneurs of capitalist society produce, along with their emergence and growth, the technologists, economists, the organizers of the new culture, and the legal system. The entrepreneur represents the system in the higher realms of social activity. The entrepreneur acquires the talent for this through intellectual and leadership roles. Entrepreneurs should have the capability to play the leadership role not just in their respective fields but in all others as well, especially in those connected with economic activity. Moreover, the entrepreneurs should also earn the trust of those who invest in their enterprise and those who purchase their products.

Social organizers

Expanding this concept, Gramsci says that at least some of the top entrepreneurs should have the capability to organize the entire society. The best among them should be capable of establishing their hegemony over the complex network of service sectors that reach up to the level of governments or the State. Only through this can the entrepreneurs create circumstances which are conducive to the growth of their class. Sections of the intellectuals of each class should have their own specialized skills and capabilities.

As an example, Gramsci points to the case of military leaders in feudal societies. The feudal lords' control over the military sustained their hegemony over society. Once this control became loose, their hegemony also started to decline. Gramsci points out that though the peasantry had played a significant role in feudal society it could neither produce its own intellectuals nor could it accommodate the traditional intellectuals.

It has to be noted that the role of military officials in feudal societies is not directly applicable to India. For the feudal system which came into being in Italy or other European societies was not similar to that which was present in India. However, the hegemony enjoyed by the upper castes of India's caste hierarchy was significant. The role played in India's history by those who invaded northern India and set up empires and those foreigners who arrived for trade in other parts of the country is very important.

The upper and subsidiary social castes, the Persian-Turco-Mongol rulers, and the foreign traders could collectively provide a firm basis for establishing a caste-landlord-feudal hegemony in India from one end to the other. The intellectuals of this system could make great contributions to Sanskrit, Pali, and Persian literatures. The large empire and its administrative as well as military establishment came into being in the political and policy spheres.

This system was brought down by the British traders and their administrators. The British dominance led to Indians 'losing [their] old world without gaining the new', as Marx wrote. He pointed out that although Indians could not gain a new world, a new breed of intellectuals working for the creation of a new India rose from within the English-established system. Through this process had emerged the Indian nationalist movement and the two classes that formed it – namely the bourgeoisie and the proletariat.

Religious leaders and intellectuals

Each class that exists in a prevailing social system would find its own intellectual section and rear it to suit its own interests. A classic example of this according to Gramsci is the Christian religious establishment of Italy in particular and Europe in general. The religious leaders of these regions had played a commanding role not just in the realm of religious ideas, philosophy or the State but in the fields of education, morality, jurisprudence, humanitarian activities, etc. as well. They could get along well with the feudal landlords and had enjoyed various privileges connected to private property. Since this system's ideological basis was the Christian faith, these religious leaders had emerged as the spokespersons of an idealist philosophy. Gramsci provides many examples to illustrate this. In order to produce a new generation of intellectuals, it should be understood that though no human is devoid of intellectual elements, everyone is not able to deliver the function of intellectuals.

> The problem of creating a new stratum of intellectuals consists therefore in the critical elaboration of the intellectual activity that exists in everyone at a certain degree of development, modifying its relationship with the muscular-nervous effort towards a new equilibrium . . . (*Prison Notebooks*, p. 9)

Until recently, intellectuals were thought to be only writers, philosophers, artistes, journalists, etc. But today, technical education linked to industrial production has become the basis for producing new intellectuals. (It is in this perspective that Gramsci deals with the problems of education which is the second chapter in *Prison Notebooks*.)

Consent and force

Gramsci's Marxist-Leninist perspective on intellectuals led him to study the problems of the mutual relations of the State and civil society. The relations between intellectuals and the capitalist system are not direct but manifest themselves through different forms in the upper structure of society. They can be understood only by grasping the links and differences between a civil society that functions almost independently and the ruling State that uses force on the ruled. Civil society is organized on the basis of the general consent that the ruling class enjoys from people. On the other hand, the State chooses to employ force mostly in matters in which people do not enjoy consent. In both cases, the leadership is with the ruling class. But in civil society, the class enjoys nearly complete consent of the majority of people. It is when this consent starts to disappear that the State exerts increasing force in order to subordinate the people. The intellectuals of the bourgeoisie succeed in helping deliver both these functions. According to Gramsci, unless the subordinate classes bring up their own intellectuals, they will not succeed in resisting the civil society or the State led by the dominant classes.

Towns and villages

Although intellectuals in urban areas grow along with industrial development, they have no autonomous existence. Industrial growth is planned and executed by capitalist leaders, who draw in the urban intellectual to assist them in this task.

The intellectuals in villages work with the rural masses and perform their traditional role. They have relations with the peasant masses as well as the *petite bourgeoisie* of the towns. Living in rural areas and working as lawyers and so on, they have social and political significance too. Their profession can hardly be delinked from their political function.

Those rural folk who engage in the intellectual professions of priest, lawyer, teacher, doctor, and so on enjoy a better standard of living than the rest of the villagers. This prompts the ordinary rural folk to look upon intellectuals as a model in order to improve their own miserable lives. The peasant always wants at least one of their children to become an intellectual, especially a priest. They hope that it will help them improve their family's economic and social status.

However, the peasants' attitude towards the rural intellectual has two diverse characteristics which often appear even contradictory. Even as the peasants generally respect the intellectuals' – especially the State employees' – social status, the peasants also nurse elements of contempt, envy, or even anger towards them. Nothing can be understood about the collective life of the peasantry without examining in depth the contours of their 'effective subordination' to the intellectuals.

But the status of the urban intellectuals is different. The technicians working in factories are unable to execute any political function over the workers and staff there. On the contrary, the intellectuals who rise from the workers are capable of exerting political influence on the technicians.

Role of Political Parties

Following the description of the differences and relations between urban- and rural-type intellectuals, Gramsci begins a discussion on the role of modern political parties.

Firstly, for certain social groups, a political party is specifically intended to formulate their own category of intellectuals. For them a party is a medium to express their own identity in the political and philosophical fields and not just in the field of productive techniques. These groups can bring up their own intellectuals only through this way.

Secondly, a political party's function in civil society is similar to that of the State in the larger political society, for all social groups. Political parties connect the intellectuals of a dominant social group and the traditional intellectuals.

Intellectuals: Organic and Traditional

Gramsci calls *organic intellectuals* those who identify with the interests and perspectives of the class, section or alliances which take the lead in or support society's march forward. As opposed to it, the *traditional intellectuals* are those who support the status quo and the class or sections which want to sustain it. The competition and war between the organic and traditional intellectuals are key elements in the revolutionary struggle or class war. Gramsci explains:

One of the most important characteristics of any group that is developing towards dominance is its struggle to assimilate and to conquer 'ideologically' the traditional intellectuals, but this assimilation and conquest is made quicker and more efficacious the more the group in question succeeds in simultaneously elaborating its own organic intellectuals. (*Prison Notebooks*, p. 10)

Although this process is seen during times of big changes in all societies since the ancient world, its importance increased manifold in the modern period, according to Gramsci. The Renaissance, which followed the European Middle Ages (or Dark Ages), marked the beginning of the Modern Age. The phenomenal progress witnessed in education, scientific inquiry, trade, industry, and so on during this period led to a significant rise in the number and functions of intellectuals of all kinds. India witnessed a similar phase during the first decade of the 19th century. Raja Ram Mohan Roy was the great pioneer of India's own organic intellectual tradition.

Obviously, Gramsci does not deal with the Indian context. Yet he rightly pointed out that the gulf between organic intellectuals and the masses in Indian and Chinese history was much wider than in other countries. We cannot expect Gramsci to have delved further into the reasons for this predicament like the upper caste-landlord system of India or the Confucian-Mandarin hegemony in China, or the narrowing of this gulf with the advent of the *organic* intellectuals of the modern age. Well, it is the job of us Indians. Yet, undoubtedly, Gramsci has provided the direction, and the model for further inquiries in this direction, more than anyone before him.

Historical Assessment

The specific situation of each country has to be subjected to detailed examination in order to get a clear picture of the relations between the intellectuals and political parties, and also their contemporary problems. This examination was started off by Gramsci. While Gramsci's reference to India and China is incidental and insufficient, he had studied the European situation in some detail. Though hardly complete, the insights he provided are of immense value. Even though his native Italy takes priority, Gramsci did analyse and explain in brief the phenomenon of the formation of intellectuals as well as their relations with political parties and processes in other European countries, the USA, South and Central America, Japan, and so on. Notwithstanding its brevity, none other than Gramsci has as yet made a Marxist analysis of this phenomenon.

Gramsci examined the circumstances that produced the intellectuals of the Greco-Roman civilization, often called the Classical Age. How did those intellectuals relate to the slave societies of those days? Gramsci pointed out that Emperor Julius Caesar's decision to grant citizenship to doctors and others with specialist skills proves that the intellectual community was a significant group during the period. The imperial intellectuals of that age evolved to become the Roman Catholic priestly class of the feudal Middle Ages after the collapse of the empire.

Gramsci explained how the class of modern intellectuals was brought forward by the great French bourgeois-democratic revolution of 1789 and the events that had led to it. The breakdown of the relation between the Catholic Church and the political processes made way for the advent of modernity.

However, Gramsci noted how the intellectuals of England continued to remain under the influence of feudalism long after the country came under the bourgeoisie without going through a direct bourgeois revolution. In Germany, the 'Junkers' (landlords) became industrialists without abandoning their interests in land. The sway of Junkers continued over German intellectuals until Germany was defeated in the First World War even as the period witnessed the growth of the proletariat and its own intellectuals.

Gramsci examined how historic events like the emergence of the Byzantine Empire, the Norman attack, the entry of the Greek Orthodox Church, and so on, had transformed the Russian intellectual realm. The experience of the USA, which was formed by the new emigrants who carried no baggage of the past, was different from all these countries. The class of traditional intellectuals assumed no relevance in the early days of the USA. Yet, the class of Black intellectuals who emerged from the Afro-American community in the USA was a phenomenon similar to developments in other countries. Thus, although not very comprehensive, Gramsci's *Prison Notebooks* marked a beginning in the examination of the growth of intellectuals and political parties on the basis of a Marxist-Leninist understanding. It is the duty of Marxist-Leninists in all countries to put to practice Gramsci's methodology in accordance with the context of their respective country.

Chapter 10

PHILOSOPHY OF EDUCATION

This is in a way an extension of Gramsci's chapter on the intellectuals. The right education system is imperative to creating the stratum of intellectuals, for the country in general and the proletariat in particular. For today's students happen to be tomorrow's intellectuals.

Italy's educational institutions during Gramsci's time were of two kinds:

1. Traditional ('Classical') and undifferentiated institutions that impart to students their lessons on general culture and help them find by themselves a vocation and a path for future.
2. Institutions which provide specialized vocational (technological) guidance.

The first kind of institution was there to cater to the children of dominant classes and intellectuals and to provide them with general education to raise their cultural standards. The second kind was to help the lower class ('instrumental classes') acquire some technical skills to find their livelihood. 'The development of an industrial base both in the cities and countryside meant a growing need for the new type of urban intellectuals,' wrote Gramsci.

Directions for reforms

Gramsci pointed out that there was an increasing tendency to abolish traditional schools that did not serve 'immediate interests' but served only a tiny elite which does not have to worry about a livelihood. 'Instead, there is a steady growth of specialized vocational schools, in which the pupil's destiny and future activity are determined in advance', Gramsci wrote. He called for a rational policy to strike a balance and encourage both kinds of institutions. 'First, a common basic education, imparting a general, humanistic, formative culture; this would strike the right balance between development of the capacity for working manually (technically, industrially) and development of the capacities required for intellectual work.' He pointed out the need to encourage both kinds of institutions for the right progress of society. He also said that it was the State's role to organize educational institutions. The State should also bear the responsibility of deciding upon the number and types of intellectuals necessary for society, and organizing the schools and their infrastructure.

Two Stages

According to Gramsci, the primary grade should be of three- or four-years' duration, when pupils should be imparted the basics – reading, writing, math, geography, history, and so on. But during this period, they should also be taught their 'rights and duties', which were much neglected. This was to impart to the children the capability at this age to live as members of the civil society. The secondary stage should last six years in order to complete all the grades by the time the pupil attains the age of 15 or 16 years. He repeatedly stressed on the need to bring in creative methods of learning science and life during the last phase of school itself and to not leave it as a monopoly of university education. Gramsci called for a common school system which would instil the fundamental values of humanism, intellectual self-discipline, and moral independence, which were necessary for subsequent specialization at the university level.

This would enable the pupil to attain a higher intellectual and moral level besides fostering independent responsibility by the time he/she entered university. Instead of subjecting themselves to a discipline imposed by force, the young men and women would be self-disciplined enough to pursue the courses of their preference.

Principles of Education

Along with his suggestions related to educational reforms, Gramsci also articulated his principles on education. Traditionally, there were two elements in Italy's primary education. They were the basics of natural sciences and the idea of civic rights and duties. If these two were imparted properly, it would help keep superstition at bay. Such a development required an understanding of the relations between nature and society and practical and theoretical exercises involving teachers and students. Reading books alone is hardly sufficient to realize the objectives of education.

Secondly, it is important that the teacher understands that there is a divide between him/her and the student community. The teacher should consciously strive to bridge this gulf. It is also essential that the students' cultural levels are raised by the teacher in order to help them grow into complete human beings. The teacher has to impart new knowledge to the students with the objective of helping them grow into those capable of thinking and understanding for themselves.

Thirdly, traditional schools in Italy used to teach two classical languages – Greek and Latin – together with their respective literatures and grammar. In spite of the mechanical nature of this study, it contributed to the development of the students' personality and formation of character. It was not intended to teach them to speak in these languages or for other utilitarian needs but to help them know about the civilizations of Greece and Rome. Though this learning was by mechanical repetition or rote, it was essential to inculcate in the students certain habits of diligence, precision, poise, and the ability to concentrate on specific subjects. Mental-physical habits acquired through disciplined and mechanical coercion in younger days help scholars acquire more knowledge by themselves later.

It is clear that Gramsci dealt with issues related to education as a medium to develop intellectuals not just good for the nation but for the working class as well.

Chapter 11

THE INTERNATIONAL

REVOLUTIONARY MOVEMENT

'Notes on Italian History' was the title of the third chapter of Gramsci's *Prison Notebooks*. However, it deals only with Italian history of the 19th and 20th centuries. Yet, the chapter contains a narrative of the history of Europe. European history of this age is closely linked to the history of humanity and hence this article is captioned 'The International Revolutionary Movement'.

According to the editor of *Prison Notebooks*, Gramsci had intended to carry out a study of religious reformation and renaissance when he was planning this chapter. Gramsci thus wrote about his theoretical approach for this study:

[T]he Renaissance was a vast movement, which started after the year 1000, and of which Humanism and the Renaissance (in the narrow sense of the word) were two closing moments – moments which were primarily located in Italy, whereas the more general historical process was European and not only Italian. Humanism and the Renaissance, as the literary expression of this European historical movement, were located primarily in Italy; but the progressive movement after the year

1000, although an important part of it took place in Italy with the Communes, precisely in Italy degenerated . . . while in the rest of Europe the general movement culminated in the national states and then in the world expansion of Spain, France, England, Portugal. In Italy what corresponded to the national states of these countries was the organisation of the Papacy as an absolute state . . . which divided the rest of Italy, etc. . . . The Renaissance may be viewed as the cultural expression of an historical process in which there was created in Italy a new intellectual class of European dimensions. This class divided into two branches: one exercised a cosmopolitan function in Italy linked to the Papacy and reactionary in character; the other was formed outside Italy, from political and religious exiles, and exercised a progressive cosmopolitan function in the various countries where it existed, or participated in the organisation of the modern states as a technical element in the armed forces, in politics, in engineering, etc. (*Prison Notebooks*, p. 44)

In sum, the Renaissance movement that had its origin in Italy played a very significant role in the emergence of the nation-states with the social structure and political framework of the modern bourgeoisie. However, the national state governments that came into being in other European countries did not appear in Italy. Instead, what came was the universal authority of the Pope and the Middle Ages' imperialism based in Austria. This led to a major divide forming between Italy and the rest of Europe.

Many elements of bourgeois modernity had first emerged in European countries like Spain, England, and Portugal. The process manifested as the historic revolution of 1789 in France which had its impact on all European countries. Most European countries had fallen under Napoleon's military power which represented the French revolution. The nationalist resistance against the foreign army spread across borders culminating in Napoleon's defeat. As mentioned earlier, this process led to national governments coming to power in Spain, Portugal, France, and England. For the first time in history each nationality came to have its own country and government in Europe.

Yet these events had left Italy untouched. It was not a country of a nationality, but part of the German empire centred in Austria. Moreover, it was the Pope's regressive cultural system that philosophically as well as religiously dominated the region.

It was for liberation from this that the progressives of Italy had waged a struggle for national unification. The unification movement's objectives were to liberate Italy from its state of being a vassal to Austrian imperialism, and the formation of a nation-state by amalgamating all the Italian regions. Although there was a parallel wing of progressives within this movement, it worked under the leadership of the moderates. The emergence of a widespread Left movement as part of the French Revolution did not occur in Italy.

Left groups had made leeway in most of the revolutions that occurred during the decades between 1830 and 1860 in various European countries. The communist movements which came into being in some of these countries under the leadership of Marx and Engels were part of this Left advance. In Italy, even the radical groups which had Left characteristics were under moderate bourgeois leadership. This left Italy behind other European countries in the emergence of Left democratic movements.

Gramsci was prompted to tell this story by exploring the emergence of the reactionary wave that had swept across Italy and other European countries in the aftermath of the First World War – when Mussolini's Fascism and Hitler's Nazism rose in Italy and Germany respectively which went on to repress the revolutionary proletarian movements. Gramsci resolved to conduct a detailed study of the phenomenon.

As part of this project, Gramsci and other Italian Communist leaders decided to carry out a historical analysis which, though focused on Italy in particular, would have relevance for all of Europe, and also the world in general. It was mentioned earlier about the series of discussions that the Italian Communist Party and the Communist International had held on this issue. Gramsci played a crucial role in this assessment to expose the new reactionary force which posed a threat to the working class and all progressive democratic forces and also to chalk out the strategies of resistance. He made a theoretical study on the circumstances which had led to the emergence of this state only after he was imprisoned. This study is his 'Notes on Italian History' contained in the *Prison Notebooks*.

Although titled 'Notes on Italian History', Gramsci analyses the overall setback suffered by the global revolutionary movement following the French Revolution. He examines the Napoleonic campaigns in various European countries and the consequent setbacks suffered by revolutionary movements in diverse manifestations. The counter-revolutionary storm that swept across Europe following Napoleon's defeat, the revolutionary uprisings in various European countries to resist this which led to the working-class revolution of Paris in 1871, its much higher manifestation as the Russian Revolution of 1917 which in its turn unleashed a revolutionary wave across many countries and the eventual setback it suffered after a few years are then analysed by Gramsci. According to him all these were indispensable parts of the process of global revolution. A revolution followed by a counter-revolution succeeded again by another revolutionary upsurge was the order in which history advanced, says Gramsci.

Six decades after Gramsci wrote *Prison Notebooks*, the global revolutionary movement had suffered its worst setback. The Socialist bloc led by the Soviet Union faced the cataclysmic events that eventually threw them back into capitalism. This had immediately prompted the enemies of socialism to shout from the rooftops that socialism was all over, and capitalism had attained its final victory. Gramsci's analysis that the history of humanity's advance was through the alternate stages of revolution, counter-revolution and newer revolutions is the fitting response to these prophets of doom.

It's true that Marx, Engels and Lenin too had pointed to these historical processes. But it was essential to enrich this thesis in the backdrop of the counter-revolution that followed the Russian Revolution of 1917. It was incumbent on Italy's proletarian intellectuals to carry out this task since that country was one of the worst victims of counter-revolution. This is the significance of Gramsci's 'Notes on Italian History'.

Gramsci's findings assume exceptional significance not only in a historical context but also as a text for revolutionary strategy. For they form a guide to the strategies proletarian revolutionaries should adopt when counter-revolutionary storms sweep the interregnum between two revolutions.

Two negative tendencies are likely to appear in the working-class revolutionary movements in the circumstances of counter-revolution. Gramsci warns against both. One is to continue with the same strategies (offensive) adopted during the revolutionary upsurge without understanding that counter-revolution has triumphed. The other is to surrender to the counter-revolution without recognizing its internal contradictions that would lead to another revolutionary stage. Gramsci points out that both of these are wrong and underscores the need to make preparations for yet another revolutionary advance even when counter-revolution is at its height.

Gramsci borrows a wartime strategy to be adopted in these circumstances. Understand clearly the power of the enemy and lie low patiently until circumstances turn favourable to launch the counter-offensive. All these steps – launching the offensive, waiting with patience, preparing for future – form different stages of the revolutionary process.

Launching the offensive was crucial when revolutions had swept countries like England, Holland, among others, in the 17th and 18th centuries. So was the case during the French Revolution of 1789 and other European revolutions of 1848 and 1871. When counter-revolution followed these revolutions, it was time for waiting and preparing. Offence became the strategy again during the Russian Revolution in 1917. But patient waiting became imperative when fascism rose in Italy and other European nations. Gramsci's *Notes* were written during this period.

The offensive was launched before long as per the policy adopted by the Seventh Congress of the International which culminated in the triumph against fascism. This was followed by the period of waiting and preparing in order to counter the enemy's Cold War strategies. Today, when the Socialist bloc has suffered a major setback, the strategy to be adopted is to wait and prepare for the next offensive.

The strategy Gramsci has developed is significant both as theory as well as practice. He elaborates this further in subsequent writings too.

It could be dismissed as nothing new but only an elaboration of what Marx, Engels, and Lenin had formulated. Yet Gramsci's work assumes importance as an objective analysis of the major setback suffered by global Socialism and also for expanding the concepts formulated by Marx, Engels and Lenin in order to deal with new circumstances.

Chapter 12

THE MODERN PRINCE

As pointed out earlier, Italy did not experience the authoritarianism of modern royal rule, which was witnessed in other European countries such as Spain, France, and England. Machiavelli's political treatise *The Prince* called for Italy to go through this stage in history. The work is the treatise of royal authoritarianism. Gramsci takes the concept of 'the Prince' in this work in order to associate it with modern capitalism. He suggests that the collective leadership of the proletariat would emerge from struggles within capitalism. Gramsci calls Marx the theoretician of this transition. A section in Gramsci's work is even titled 'Machiavelli and Marx'. According to him, they are the theoreticians of two kinds of revolutionary politics. Machiavelli was the theorist of the bourgeois revolution, and Marx was the theorist of proletarian revolutionary politics.

Like Machiavelli's Prince, Marx too demonstrates a model for revolutionary leadership. But unlike the singular valiant hero like the Machiavellian Prince, Marx's proletarian leader is the collective movement formed by the oppressed millions led by the modern working class and represented by its political party.

As in most of Gramsci's articles in *Prison Notebooks*, he does not appear very candid on this topic. The reason could be that Gramsci was incarcerated while he drafted these texts, and it could be that his forte was theoretical analysis. Gramsci's conduct as a practical activist during his pre-prison times had given way to that of a philosopher in *Prison Notebooks*.

However, Marxist philosophers are not supposed to just interpret the world, but to strive to transform it. Hence Gramsci's method of philosophical analysis is always interspersed with contemporary political practice.

Dual characteristics of authority

Gramsci's exploration into political philosophy begins with a focus on the fundamental differences between the mutual relationship of the rulers and the ruled as against that of the political leadership and its followers. Gramsci points out that the influence exerted by the rulers on the ruled is different from that by the political leaders on their ranks. The hallmark of the former is the use of force.

The dominant class that is in power exerts force on its adversaries. For instance, the ruling apparatus of a bourgeois society uses force against its feudal adversaries on the one side and the poor on the other. Hence Marx and Engels said that bourgeois democracy is authoritarianism in the final analysis.

The poor millions and the proletariat which leads them also employ all methods of resistance including the use of force against their bourgeois adversaries during the time when they work for the victory of the revolution. The working class in no country would follow the theory of non-violence preached by people like Tolstoy or Gandhi during its political struggle against the bourgeoisie. Once it comes to power after the revolutionary victory over the bourgeoisie, the new State of the working class does not hesitate to suppress with force all attempts by the dethroned ruling classes to rise again. Hence, Marx and Engels called the State that comes after revolution the 'dictatorship of the proletariat'.

Be it bourgeois rule or proletarian dictatorship, no ruling class of any age would exert force on its allies. They take on adversaries by keeping their allies within the fold through ideological campaigns and debates on contemporary issues. Hence, it is integral to the dictatorship of the proletariat to build alliances of labourers and peasants.

The concept of 'democratic centralism' within the Party has to be seen in this context. It is derived from the perfect balance of a rigorous centralized leadership and the broad-based internal democracy of the Party. Weakening of either would lead to the collapse of the organization.

It was earlier mentioned that Gramsci had been anxious about the erosion of internal democracy in the Communist International. Subsequent history proved that his anxiety was not at all unfounded. Considering the resultant setbacks faced by the global Communist movement, it has become imperative today to attach to both sides – 'dictatorship of proletariat' and 'democratic centralism' – equal importance.

Regionalism, Nationalism, Internationalism

Machiavelli's Prince gave priority to nationalism and kept regional feelings under check. But Gramsci's 'Modern Prince' integrated them to uphold the working class's concepts of nationalism and internationalism.

Its shining evidence is the birth of a global Communist movement with roots not just in Europe but spread out to Asia, Africa, and Latin America following the formation of the Third International. The First and Second Internationals had remained within the confines of Europe. Gramsci had lived during the nascent years of this new era. He had completed nine years in prison by the time the Communist movement became a global force and breathed his last after two more years.

Today, neither the Communist International nor the Soviet Union – both symbols of the global working-class movement – exist. Opponents cry aloud that global Communism is dead and gone. Besides, various kinds of sinister and sectarian forces, including those of ultra-provincialism, are gathering strength in the former Soviet republics, former Socialist countries of Eastern Europe, and also various other parts of Western Europe and even in India.

Nevertheless, there are attempts under way globally to rebuild the progressive forces and overcome these divisive and sectarian trends. The concept of unity between the working class and other suffering masses propounded by Marx and Engels and developed subsequently by Lenin is increasingly gathering strength. This emerging force is Gramsci's *Modern Prince.*

There could be setbacks to its course forward. Yet, overcoming these obstacles, the Modern Prince (the revolutionary political leadership of the proletariat) is moving forward, optimistic about the emergence of a universal humanism constituting working-class internationalism that integrates national liberation and unity with due recognition of the regional identities within.

The poor, the working class and the Party

Before concluding this brief note on the *Modern Prince,* another issue has to be addressed; the relationship between the Party and the working class on the one hand, and that between the working class and the poor masses on the other.

Leaders of the world revolutionary movement, starting from Marx, Engels, and Lenin, have repeatedly emphasized one cardinal point: that revolution is conducted not by one bright leader or a group of bright leaders but by the common masses. Revolution would succeed only when the will and capability of the masses grow and gather critical strength. No revolution will succeed without mass participation on a large scale.

The Russian Revolution of 1917 was the product of the revolutionary fervour and capability of the workers, peasants, and fighters. The Chinese revolution of 1949 was successfully organized by the starving millions in the countryside led by the workers and intellectuals from towns.

Gramsci pointed out that the Italian revolution would succeed only through the revolutionary alliance between the working-class leadership from the factory councils and the poor masses from the rural countryside.

In order to put this Marxist-Leninist principle into practice it is essential to unleash the revolutionary strength of the poor masses. It is also important that the militant organizations of the toiling masses in both the rural and urban areas function with autonomy. Even as the working-class Party gives it ideological and political leadership, those fighting sections of the poor masses should be ensured sufficient autonomy in functioning.

The Party should be capable of understanding the direction taken by the revolutionary movement. It should also take the initiative to educate the people. It should also take care not be a stumbling block to the unleashing of the revolutionary force of the poor masses. Gramsci points out three things required in the Party.

1. An organization of activists committed to utmost discipline and class loyalty. This is imperative for the very survival of the Party.
2. A centralized leadership that coordinates the revolutionaries and keeps them within the organization without which it would be an army without a commander.
3. A decisive middle-level leadership that functions between these two entities.

Objective circumstances and subjective forces

Even in the presence of these three factors, revolutionary activities would be possible only in a revolutionary environment which would be intense enough to animate the masses. This environment would not materialize with the will of the leaders alone or even of the Party as a whole. Objective circumstances have to develop that favour the onset of revolution. The revolutionary organization of the working class stands out from other parties with the capability to study the formation of such objective circumstances and understand its distinct features.

The working-class leadership should have from the beginning a clear understanding of the direction in which the objective circumstances lead. It was on account of this understanding that the revolutions of Russia, China, Vietnam, Korea, and Cuba could take place.

It was the inability to analyse the objective circumstances and take the revolution in the right direction that had led to the setbacks suffered by Socialism in Soviet Union and other East European countries. It was a far better understanding that prevented such a predicament in countries like Vietnam, Korea, and Cuba.

It is obvious that over and above merely learning the works of Marx, Engels, or Lenin by rote, the Marxist-Leninist leadership should be capable of understanding their spirit and putting them into practice according to the specific concrete circumstances of their respective country. As Lenin says, Marxism is an attempt to find solutions by subjecting concrete circumstances to a concrete examination.

Gramsci's most significant contribution is that he could successfully attempt this in his own country even after the failure of the revolution. This is clearly evident in all his presentations in the *Prison Notebooks.*

Chapter 13

FASCISM AGAINST WORLD REVOLUTION

The second and highly important chapter in Gramsci's *Notes on Politics* (*Prison Notebooks*, pp. 123–220) is titled 'State and Civil Society'. Civil society's attempt is to bring about a consensus among the public through social organizations, cultural organizations including those linked to religion, class organizations of labourers and peasants, and political parties. It is when this attempt fails that the State comes into play by making use of its coercive machinery such as the police, the army, or the prisons.

Both civil society and State have a similar class character. Both are headed by exploiting classes. Both are in opposition to the large majority of people. But there is one difference between these two. The exploiters use peaceful methods to impose their hegemony over the masses, while the State uses force. In short, both civil society and the State are weapons of exploiters.

The dynamics of both are regulated by the laws of dialectical and historical materialism. Exacerbation of the contradictions between opposing classes in society or within the exploiting classes could lead to a situation where the existing class society cannot continue any longer. It is at this juncture that the exploiting classes abandon the means of peace for the use of force.

Even this might prove to fail. The exploiters' attempts to

resort to force could be collectively resisted by the exploited through peaceful means or even force. This leads to the outbreak of revolution.

Citing examples of this, Gramsci writes about Gandhi's struggles too. He pointed out that the Gandhian struggle against the British had three aspects. One, self-protection. An example of this aspect was the boycott of imported products. The second was direct agitation like organizing strikes. Finally, the collection of arms. (Though the last was not part of Gandhian struggles, Gramsci included this too as it was a routine activity organized by nationalist revolutionaries in parallel to the non-violent methods.)

Like the Gandhian modes of struggle, Gramsci has also mentioned certain revolutionary methods which were practised in Germany and other European countries. They are basically those struggles which manifest at the height of the class war.

Caesarism, Bonapartism, Fascism

Gramsci has given three examples in history when circumstances led to the State resorting to violence.

1. Caesarism or Julius Caesar's authoritarian rule in ancient Rome.
2. The first stage of Bonapartism and its two subsequent versions that came into being under Napoleon Bonaparte following the French Revolution of 1789.
3. European fascism created by the bourgeoisie to suppress the sweeping revolutionary wave triggered by the Russian Revolution of 1917.

While discussing each of these, Gramsci analyses the political circumstances which led to them. As social conflicts in general and class contradictions in particular approach a climax, the existing social structure collapses; yet, a political force which is capable of replacing those who sit on top of the collapsing structure and take over does not emerge. In these circumstances emerges a leader who is capable of rallying the masses behind him.

This leader exerts influence, positioned between the different ruling classes and warring social classes. This was how Caesar or Bonaparte, or Fascism had emerged in different periods in history. It would be an oversimplification to refer to all these phenomena as merely authoritarian regimes. They should be seen as expressions of exacerbating social contradictions.

According to Gramsci, Caesarism, and Bonapartism played conflicting roles in different periods in history. The historical roles of Caesar and Bonaparte (in the first stage) were to strengthen the progressive social forces of their respective periods. However, Bonaparte's role in the subsequent stages and the European fascism that followed the Russian revolution were exactly to the contrary, since they backed the reactionary forces to destroy progressive social forces.

The new stage

The conflict between the reactionary and progressive social forces has reached a new stage with the advent of the revolutionary movement of the modern proletariat. A strategy of proletarian movement came into being consisting of class and mass organizations, political parties which lead them, newspapers and other mass media forms to propagate ideas, and the parliamentary methods which would cleverly combine all the above.

In these circumstances emerges the working-class party which Gramsci called the 'Modern Prince' in place of 'valiant heroes' like Caesar or Bonaparte. The revolutionary leadership of the proletariat emerges instead of Bonapartism which plays only a limited progressive role. There could also be the formation of a collective Bonapartism under the revolutionary classes and masses. As Marx and Engels wrote in the *Communist Manifesto*, 'All previous historical movements were movements of minorities, or in the interests of minorities. The proletarian movement is the self-conscious, independent movement of the immense majority, in the interest of the immense majority.'

World working-class revolutionary movement

It was to realize this vision that the First International was initiated by Marx and Engels, the Second International under Engels's active leadership, and the Third International under Lenin. This led to the world proletarian movement becoming an organized force. The process of constructing a socialist society was afoot at least in one country – Russia. Inspired by the Soviet society's achievements, masses in various countries under imperialist hegemony began resistance movements aimed at social revolution.

Fascism, which began in Italy and acquired diabolical form in Germany, was a major stage in this process. The Seventh Congress (1935) of the Communist International was entrusted with the responsibility of rallying the masses against Fascism.

Gramsci was in prison during that period. However, as mentioned earlier, he had taken this stance even before the International took this decision. Gramsci wrote his opinion on certain issues in his *Notes on Politics* which triggered controversy inside the Third International. They may be summarized as follows:

1. An intense debate had occurred between Lenin and Rosa Luxemburg over the question of the role of the party leadership when – in revolutionary conditions – the masses actively participate in agitations. Rosa's approach was to attach more importance to the evolution of the revolutionary circumstances, and less to the direct role

of the party. Gramsci clarified that he agreed more with Lenin than Rosa in this debate.

2. The relationship between nationalism and internationalism had raised a sharp debate within the Soviet Communist Party and also in the Communist International. While Stalin's approach was based on nationalism, Trotsky stood for internationalism. Gramsci held that the revolution's future vision should be international although nationalism had a much more significant role in the short run than Trotsky ascribed to it. Besides, he believed that Trotsky's idea of 'immediate world revolution' was hardly practical.

3. Trotsky also had the idea of 'permanent revolution' that would never come to end with the establishment of socialism in one country alone but continue until the complete liquidation of the reactionary forces. This concept was diametrically antithetical to Marxism-Leninism. Marxism saw revolution as a process that moves forward and backwards continuously. Hence the proletarian party has to adopt different strategies for times of progress and reaction. As Gramsci pointed out, even when the revolution suffers setback, work should be afoot to prepare for future stages of advancement. This was as important a strategy as making maximum utility of the stages of advancement. Trotsky's prescription would surely lead to left-wing sectarianism.

It is clear from this that Gramsci was against Trotsky and with Stalin on the issues that rocked the Soviet party during those days. However, as mentioned earlier, Gramsci had serious apprehensions about Stalin's leadership on issues of inner-party democracy. Gramsci breathed his last before his apprehensions became an enormous reality.

It has been six decades since Gramsci wrote the *Prison*

Notebooks. It was written when Gramsci's personal life as well as the Italian Communist Party and the Communist International were passing through a profound crisis. Gramsci was in prison and so unhealthy that there was no hope of ever returning to a normal life even after his release. The Italian Communist Party was living through a period of unprecedented repression. Grave problems were on the rise in the Soviet party leadership as well as the International.

But none of this discouraged Gramsci. This is how he ends the section on 'State and Civil Society' in *Notes on Politics*, penned in prison:

[C]onditions are being created for an unprecedented expansion of historical materialism. The very poverty which at first inevitably characterises historical materialism as a theory diffused widely among the masses will help it to spread. The death of the old ideologies takes the form of scepticism with regard to all theories and general formulae ... [and points to] the possibility and necessity of creating a new culture. (*Prison Notebooks*, p. 276)

According to the fundamental principle of historical materialism, the working class and their struggles determine the direction of history. Gramsci and other prominent Marxist leaders were guided by the optimistic belief that only the common masses could and would vanquish the forces of Fascism that had gripped Italy and other capitalist countries of Europe.

Even before a decade had passed after Gramsci's death, Fascist and Nazi dominance in Italy and Germany respectively had collapsed. Anti-fascist governments had come to power not just in these two countries but in the whole of Western Europe. In the subsequent years, the European imperialist powers had to withdraw from the colonies which had been under their yoke for a long time. The conflicts between Socialism and Communism had begun to assume new forms.

These lines are being penned four decades after those days when the international revolutionary movement has come to face yet another crisis. Yet, the working people and other toiling masses all over the world have begun to prove their strength to overcome the crisis. We are now at a point in time when the optimism Gramsci expressed even at the height of fascism is of true relevance again.

Chapter 14

NEW TRENDS IN AMERICAN CAPITALISM

The last segment of Gramsci's *Notes on Politics* deals with some new trends seen in capitalism in the United States of America. Some of them had appeared in other countries too, including Italy. Yet, according to Gramsci, there was a major difference between the trends as manifested in Europe and the USA.

The struggles to uproot feudalism had not succeeded in any European country except France. Hence the parasitic classes common to feudalism were present in other European countries. In contrast, the USA never had even a trace of such classes. Here capitalism could grow into its complete form. Capitalism in the USA was marked by an efficiency that feudalism lacked.

World capitalism was passing through an unprecedentedly deep crisis in 1921. The bourgeois leaders in these countries were in search of solutions suited to each of their respective circumstances in order to overcome the crisis. If Fascism was one of those solutions found in Germany, an American way – which Gramsci called 'Fordism' – was developed in the USA.

European fascism and the new capitalist forms in the USA had a common characteristic. Direct intervention by the State in the economy came into force in both Europe and the USA. President Franklin D. Roosevelt (1882–1945) of the USA, who had initiated the policy of the State's direct intervention in the economy, called it the 'New Deal'. It was a policy that called for the government to intervene in economic affairs without weakening the democratic character of its governance system. However, the State that intervened in the economy in both USA and European countries like Italy and Germany had belonged to the big bourgeoisie. The intervention by the State in economies in even democracies like the USA was carried out in ways unacceptable not just to the ordinary people but to the small and medium-level bourgeoisie as well. Be it through unabashed fascism in Europe or the 'democratic system' in USA, the State in both the regions had paved the way for the monopoly bourgeoisie to burden the ordinary and middle classes with hardship and misery.

Lenin had analysed the process that was witnessed during the age of mutual competition in the 19th century when global capitalism was transformed into monopoly capitalism. The phenomenon of monopoly capitalism grew much more acutely by the late 1920s and 1930s. According to Marxists like Gramsci both European fascism and Americanism were attempts by the State-led monopoly capital to bring about direct intervention in the economy in order to escape the global financial crisis that came to be known as the Great Depression of the 1930s.

The New Deal launched by President Roosevelt marked a new stage in capitalism. It came to be accepted that direct intervention by the bourgeois State was essential for capitalist growth in general and to address its crisis in particular. Thus emerged the new phenomenon of *state monopoly capitalism*, which was the alliance between monopoly capital referred to by Lenin and the bourgeois State. Both bourgeois democracy and fascism were manifestations of this new phenomenon represented by President Roosevelt in USA and Hitler or Mussolini in Germany and Italy.

This new system in the USA had an economic face which Gramsci named 'Fordism'. Instead of summary rejection of workers' rights, this system recognized many of them but made them work much harder and imposed various restrictions on them. As a result, instead of workers' wages, the profits (surplus value) of the capitalist rose steeply.

While explaining this stage, Gramsci pointed out two reforms brought about in industrial areas: prohibition of the consumption of alcohol and restrictions on sexual activity. Both were intended to increase workers' productivity. Increase in the productivity of machines as well as workers would help raise the *surplus value*. A system also emerged by which to measure workers' daily input of work and to fix wage rates accordingly. Workers' conditions of wage and service were improved to provide the social background for the major increase in productivity and profit.

This system helped the USA achieve a much more efficient industrial sector than that in Europe. The efficiency in the USA came to be recognized widely in Europe too. (Even Stalin famously observed that the communist style of action should be the right mix of Russia's revolutionary vigour and US efficiency.) Obviously, it was the United States which put to work the most efficient way out from the global financial crisis. There were attempts to improve efficiency in countries like Germany too. But the new corporate system evolved in Fascist Italy and the Nazi economic reforms in Germany, which brought about many changes in the capitalist labour system, were part of preparations for the war. It was not the intention of the capitalist reforms of USA initiated under politicians like Roosevelt or industrialists like Henry Ford (1863–1947) to favour the workers. Moreover, as in Germany, the reforms in the USA also helped monopolists establish their authority over the economy as well as over the administration. State capitalism came into being in countries preparing for war as well as those which were supposedly pursuing peaceful economic advancement.

The era of State capitalism and its ways of distributing privileges to a minority of workers was in a nascent stage at the time Gramsci was writing these notes. This phenomenon was developed during and also after the war by the post-war Socialist governments that came into being under the right-wing Social Democratic parties. This also led to the growing impression that the differences between Capitalism and Socialism were narrowing. Leaders of bourgeois governments and Social Democratic parties had unleashed a tirade against Marxism-Leninism and the advance towards communism. The conflict between Capitalism and Socialism came to acquire an economic, political as well as ideological basis. Gramsci had passed away by the time this conflict began to aggravate. However, Gramsci's original analysis about the emergence and character of Americanism throws much light on the global ideological struggle that took place after his time. Gramsci examined Americanism and Fordism in the light of Lenin's observation that the achievement in the levels of production determined the victor in the global struggle between Capitalism and Socialism.

The new economic programme initiated by the Soviet Union since 1928 was proving to be much more successful in improving production and productivity in comparison to the capitalist world. Gramsci pointed out that Fordism's importance was as capitalism's new experiment to prove its efficiency vis-à-vis the Soviet system.

Gramsci's analysis was a warning that the Socialist world would be pushed behind if it did not recognize the new US experiment and formulate suitable responses to it. The subsequent 'scientific and technological revolution' that gave Capitalism an upper hand has proved this warning true. Today, we know that it was the failure to see this warning and act accordingly that had led to the setback suffered by global Socialism in the 1980s.

Chapter 15

THE STUDY OF PHILOSOPHY

We have so far given summaries of the first two sections – *Problems of History and Culture* and *Notes on Politics* – from Gramsci's *Prison Notebooks*. Now let's examine the third section – *The Philosophy of Praxis* – which contains his philosophical notes on Marxism-Leninism.

Gramsci first examines questions such as what is philosophy, how does it grow, and how it should be studied. Next is the segment on the 'Problems of Marxism'. These two together explain Gramsci's stand on dialectical and historical materialism.

Gramsci begins with the statement that it is essential to demolish the widespread prejudice that philosophy is too difficult to study. He points out that every human being is a philosopher in his or her own way or unconsciously. An ordinary person's philosophical perspective contains the following elements: the language that gives form to their ideas and concepts, their common sense, and the popular religion they profess and practise. Their beliefs, superstitions, opinions, ways of seeing things, and of acting – all these constitute ordinary folks' philosophy. Hence Gramsci says everybody is a philosopher.

Yet, there is a segment of intellectuals who subject philosophy to much deeper study and analysis than ordinary humans.

Gramsci calls them 'specialist philosophers' or philosophers of philosophers. It is important to understand the similarities and differences between these two sections. However, the specialist's philosophy cannot exist without the ordinary people's philosophical positions. The intellectual world of philosophy could be built only by processing and elevating the raw philosophical expressions of the ordinary people.

Gramsci makes another important point that philosophy, be it of ordinary people or of the intellectuals, comes into being and grows through interacting with practical life and activities. Those ordinary people who have a crude perspective on natural phenomena react to them accordingly. 'Philosophers of the philosophers' too react to them according to their perspectives. The consequences of these reactions lead to alterations in the natural phenomena. At the same time, those intellectuals and the ordinary folk who transform natural phenomena themselves undergo a transformation during the process.

Human beings – both the philosophers and the ordinary folk – who make use of natural phenomena for their own needs, come to acquire during this process more knowledge about nature and also the ability to transform it.

Gramsci points out another point in this context. The knowledge and ability to alter nature are not acquired just by individuals. Groups of these individuals, communities, anthropological categories, countries, governments, and so on too have their own respective perspectives. They come to know nature better, become able to alter it, and transform themselves in the process.

Hence, there is nothing like a philosophy common to all. Each section of society has its own philosophical perspective. An attempt to formulate a global philosophy by amalgamating different perspectives has been launched only since the emergence and growth of the capitalist society.

A common philosophical perspective that belonged to *humanity* instead of specific anthropological categories, nations, religions, castes, or races came into force for the first time in Europe during the 19th century. That was the time when capitalism originated and grew in Europe as a social system and launched its campaign to bring the whole planet under its sway. The unity of humanity was the capitalist class's philosophical perspective. It was the German philosopher Hegel who gave this perspective a concrete shape.

According to Hegel, dialectical forces operate in nature, society, and thought. It is through the mutual conflict between these forces that nature, humans, and their thinking advance. This was the basis of Hegel's dialectics. Hegel believed it would bring in the advance of all of humanity irrespective of differences between anthropological categories, classes, nations, religions, and races.

The same century witnessed the emergence of another philosophy which was based on the Hegelian perspective, but which negated its effects. Marxism was simultaneously an extension as well as a rejection of Hegelian dialectics.

Marx had accepted the Hegelian view that progress would take place through the dialectical conflict between opposing forces. However, Marx replaced the idealistic basis of Hegelian dialectics with a materialistic foundation. In Marx's own words, he 'stood Hegel on his head'. Marx put forward some other original formulations as well. They include the following: 'As philosophy finds its material weapon in the proletariat, so the proletariat finds its spiritual weapon in philosophy,' wrote Marx. Thus, in spite of its roots in Hegelianism, Marx developed dialectical materialism in its negation and converted it into the theoretical weapon of the working class.

Marx said famously, 'Philosophers have hitherto only *interpreted* the world in various ways; the point is to *change* it.' It was based on this Marxist concept that Gramsci called dialectical and historical materialism 'the philosophy of revolutionary praxis'. The unbreakable link between theory and practice was the cornerstone of Marxism.

Marx pointed out that, in concrete terms, the revolutionary process of changing the world meant replacing the exploitative system by a free society liberated from exploitation. An egalitarian society (a new communist society) would finally emerge after the passage of various stages like slavery, feudalism, and capitalism.

According to Marx, the harbinger of this change would be the working class. Like capitalism, its opponent – the proletariat – too is a global force. Hence Marx and Engels called the working class the grave-diggers of capitalism, which was the last of the exploitative systems.

Marx and Engels, who arrived at this formulation, were not merely pedantic theoreticians. Even as they gave shape to the philosophy of the proletariat, they were also in the forefront in organizing the working class as a revolutionary force.

They also elevated the modern working class which had remained largely within Europe into a globally organized revolutionary political force through the formation of the Communist League, as well as the First and Second Internationals.

Subsequently, Lenin and his successors succeeded in organizing the European working class and its allies in the poverty-stricken Afro-Asian continents into a coordinated global revolutionary political force.

The following chapter summarizes the second part of the philosophical notes which narrate the problems faced by Marxism-Leninism that gave birth to this revolutionary political force during the two decades that followed the revolution in tsarist Russia.

Chapter 16

AGAINST VULGAR MARXISM

The second essay in the section *The Philosophy of Praxis*, which is the last in the *Prison Notebooks*, is titled 'Problems of Marxism'. Here, Gramsci examines some of the contemporary debates held in the realm of philosophical discourse.

Gramsci was prompted to write this by the rise of various strands opposed to historical and dialectical materialism and the need to fight them. Theoretical dogmatism and mechanistic interpretations were spreading in the name of Marxism and dialectical and historical materialism.

Gramsci critically examines these trends and also seeks to expose the Soviet theoretician Nikolai Bukharin's arguments which formed a manifestation of a vulgar and positivist interpretation of Marxism.

Marxism's indebtedness to English political economy, German Idealist philosophy (Hegelianism), and the political heritage of the French Revolution is quite significant. Marx not only had imbibed each of them but also elevated them to be part of the new philosophical tradition of the working class.

However, these three streams do not stand in isolation in Marx's discourse. He synthesized them to develop a comprehensive vision of the working class which could be called the 'philosophy of praxis'. Thus, Marx could develop the working class's strength in order to fight the bourgeoisie not just in the economic and political spheres but in the realm of theory as well.

Even Marx and Engels who developed such a holistic worldview had to raise their voice against the young Marxists who tried to misinterpret their views. It was in this context that Marx once had famously remarked that 'if their politics represented Marxism, I am not a Marxist'. Marx and Engels carefully examined the revolutions that occurred in France and Germany and explained how various economic, political, and theoretical aspects were at work in each of them. With this perspective, they also studied the political developments in Italy, Spain, England, and the USA. They researched the socio-political situations and changes in Asian countries like India, China, Persia, and Turkey. The corpus of these studies has been referred to by later Marxists as a 'concrete examination of concrete circumstances'. Gramsci points to this as the root of Marxist wisdom. Engels wrote extensively, exposing the vulgar and mechanistic misinterpretation of Marxism which had held that the conflicts occurring in the economic realm would automatically reflect in political revolutions.

The core of Marxism is the unbreakable relation between theory and practice. Therefore, the revolutionary activities following Marxist theory need not always be correct and smooth but are beset with various pitfalls and setbacks. For social and political structures can hardly be analysed with perfect precision. Certain trends which become visible need not reach their logical completion. Social and political changes are too complex to be subjected to precise analysis unlike the experiments and results in natural sciences. It is not possible to precisely predict whether a particular economic force that functions in a particular manner would lead to any particular political change. Such mechanistic claims are alien to true Marxist perspectives.

It is in this perspective that Gramsci critically analysed

Bukharin's book, *Historical Materialism: A System of Sociology*. He accused Bukharin of having carried out a dogmatic and mechanistic interpretation of materialism, instead of viewing social forces in concrete terms.

Lenin was alive when Bukharin's book was published. In his letter written a few months before his death addressed to the Central Committee members, Lenin had both praised and criticized Bukharin in his characteristic style. Much as he lauded Bukharin's knowledge of theoretical issues, Lenin pointed out that he had not quite understood dialectics. Gramsci's critique of Bukharin too was along these lines.

Intense differences began to surface in the Soviet party soon after Lenin's death. Lenin was aware of the growing internal issues and feared that it would even lead to a split in the party. It was this deep anxiety which found expression in the letter he wrote on his deathbed which he wanted to be read out at the Twelfth Congress of the Soviet Communist Party to be held in April 1923. Lenin exposed the flaws not of Bukharin only but Stalin too in this testament.

'Comrade Stalin, having become Secretary-General, has unlimited authority concentrated in his hands, and I am not sure whether he will always be capable of using that authority with sufficient caution,' Lenin wrote. In a postscript to this, Lenin even called for the removal of Stalin from the post of general secretary:

Stalin is too coarse and this defect, although quite tolerable within our midst and in dealing among us Communists, becomes intolerable in a Secretary-General. That is why I suggest that the comrades think about a way of removing Stalin from that post and appointing another man in his stead who in all other respects differs from Comrade Stalin in having only one advantage, namely, that of being more tolerant, more loyal, more polite and more considerate to the comrades, less capricious, etc. This circumstance may appear to be a negligible detail. But I think that from the standpoint of safeguards against a split and from the standpoint of what I wrote above about the relationship between Stalin and Trotsky it is not a [minor] detail, but it is a detail which can assume decisive importance.

However, Lenin did not have anyone to recommend as replacement for Stalin who would have his positive sides but who was also free from his darker aspects. After Lenin's death, Stalin himself came forward to step down as per the departed leader's wish. But the Central Committee could not find a suitable alternative and allowed Stalin to continue.

History proved Lenin right as what he had feared came true. Stalin grossly misused the enormous powers that he wielded. Consequently, many comrades, including Bukharin, not only faced illegal disciplinary action but were killed.

The Twentieth Congress of the Soviet party and the subsequent Central Committee meetings began the campaign to expose Stalin's wrongs. This, too, provided a pretext for the rise of contemporary revisionist trends in Soviet as well as European Communist parties. One of them was the emergence of 'Eurocommunism'. The huge blow suffered by world Socialism during the 1980s and '90s was the logical culmination of this revisionary trend.

The CPI (M)'s Fourteenth and Fifteenth Congresses called for a detailed examination of the objective historical circumstances which had led to this. This is yet to take place but let a question be posed here as a pointer to the examination. Have not the dogmatism and mechanistic attitudes that Lenin and Gramsci found in Bukharin been visible in many of Lenin's successors like Stalin and others? Didn't Lenin's successors abandon his dialectical materialist position on the Soviet Union and the future of world revolution to take a dogmatic approach when implementing the

New Economic Policy? Wasn't this the cause for the events that occurred subsequently?

Lenin was aware that though the Soviet Union was capable of building socialism in tsarist Russia, it would not be able to complete the process single-handedly. For the very survival of the Soviet Union was of crucial significance in the course of mutual conflict between the capitalist and socialist worlds. Lenin was certain that although the Soviet Union could thwart the initial imperialist assault against it – the interventionist war and civil unrest – the final victory was still afar. Lenin had pointed out that Socialism would win globally against Capitalism only if it could surpass it in the field of economic production.

Did not Stalin and his successors abandon this historical and dialectical materialist position, driven by the futile hope that socialism could not just be built in the country but that it could even move towards establishing communism by merely overtaking the capitalist world in the military and diplomatic spheres? Weren't national resources essential for economic production diverted for military purposes? Was it not the reason why the Soviet Union, after having overtaken the capitalist world in economic growth during the first three decades following the revolution, began to fall behind from the 1970s?

Let's return to the new ways of US capitalism as mentioned by Gramsci in his *Prison Notebooks*. He had pointed out that while Fascism was reigning in Italy and Germany, the USA was involved in experimenting with innovative ways in the realm of economic production. According to Gramsci, US capitalism's new ways were as dangerous to the world working class as the Fascist advance in Europe.

These questions pertain to the developments in international politics of the half century following Lenin's death. Gramsci's *Prison Notebooks* is an exceptional tool to examine the setbacks faced by the world Socialist movement in the last two decades of the 20th century. The work helps the working class adopt the correct revolutionary position without swaying to either the Left or the Right.